New Directions for
Student Services

Elizabeth J. Whitt
EDITOR-IN-CHIEF

John H. Schuh
ASSOCIATE EDITOR

Research-Driven Practice in Student Affairs: Implications from the Wabash National Study of Liberal Arts Education

Georgianna L. Martin
Michael S. Hevel

EDITORS

Number 147 • Fall 2014
Jossey-Bass
San Francisco

RESEARCH-DRIVEN PRACTICE IN STUDENT AFFAIRS: IMPLICATIONS FROM THE
WABASH NATIONAL STUDY OF LIBERAL ARTS EDUCATION
Georgianna L. Martin, Michael S. Hevel (eds.)
New Directions for Student Services, no. 147

Elizabeth J. Whitt, Editor-in-Chief
John H. Schuh, Associate Editor

NEW DIRECTIONS FOR STUDENT SERVICES (ISSN 0164-7970, e-ISSN 1536-
0695) is part of The Jossey-Bass Higher and Adult Education Series and
is published quarterly by Wiley Subscription Services, Inc., A Wiley Company, at Jossey-Bass, One Montgomery Street, Suite 1200, San Francisco,
CA 94104-4594. POSTMASTER: Send address changes to New Directions
for Student Services, Jossey-Bass, One Montgomery Street, Suite 1200,
San Francisco, CA 94104-4594.

New Directions for Student Services is indexed in CIJE: Current Index to
Journals in Education (ERIC), Contents Pages in Education (T&F), Current Abstracts (EBSCO), Education Index /Abstracts (H.W. Wilson), Educational Research Abstracts Online (T&F), ERIC Database (Education
Resources Information Center), and Higher Education Abstracts (Clare-
mont Graduate University).

Microfilm copies of issues and articles are available in 16 mm and 35 mm,
as well as microfiche in 105 mm, through University Microfilms Inc., 300
North Zeeb Road, Ann Arbor, Michigan 48106-1046.

SUBSCRIPTIONS cost $89 for individuals in the U.S., Canada, and Mexico,
and $113 in the rest of the world for print only; $89 in all regions for
electronic only; and $98 in the U.S., Canada, and Mexico for combined
print and electronic; and $122 for combined print and electronic in the
rest of the world. Institutional print only subscriptions are $311 in the
U.S., $351 in Canada and Mexico, and $385 in the rest of the world; electronic only subscriptions are $311 in all regions; and combined print and
electronic subscriptions are $357 in the U.S., $397 in Canada and Mexico,
and $431 in the rest of the world.

EDITORIAL CORRESPONDENCE should be sent to the Editor-in-Chief,
Elizabeth J. Whitt, University of California Merced, 5200 North Lake Rd.
Merced, CA 95343.

www.josseybass.com

CONTENTS

Editors' Notes

Today, having a good rapport with college students and being able to plan popular programs is not enough to be considered an effective student affairs professional. Indeed, over the past two decades, student affairs professionals have faced increasing pressure to use research to inform their practice. Phrases that entered the field's lexicon representing this shift include "scholar-practitioner," "evidence-based practice," and "research-driven practice." These calls for more informed practice have occurred at the same time that student affairs practice has become more complicated. Larger numbers of students are enrolling in American higher education, these students are more diverse, the emphasis on retaining students has increased, and politicians and policymakers have called for even greater participation in higher education. As the numbers and diversity of students have expanded, student affairs professionals faced a variety of other issues that made their work more challenging, such as the explosion of technology, the growth in mental health issues, and the higher costs of attending college. Fortunately, as the call for evidence-based practice coincided within a more complicated higher education environment, the research related to higher education and student affairs has broadened.

Yet if student affairs professionals have access to more relevant scholarship, the research related to higher education and student affairs has also become increasingly complex. Acceptance rates for articles published in the field's top journals have dropped and the sophistication of statistical techniques used in these articles has increased, as *t*-tests and ANOVAs gave way to ordinal and logistic regression that are giving way to propensity scoring and multilevel modeling. And these increasingly complex statistical techniques have been accompanied by diverse forms of qualitative research that have proliferated over the past several decades.

The heightened complexity of higher education research appears, at least anecdotally, to have resulted in part from a widening divide between researchers and practitioners. In the not too distant past it was common for senior-level student affairs professionals to become faculty members in the last decade of their career, teaching and researching in graduate preparation programs. It was also relatively common for established professionals, including chief student affairs officers, to publish articles in the field's top journals. This path to the professoriate and this path to publication are increasingly rare. More often than not, individuals are deciding early on, perhaps before gaining significant practical experiences as student affairs professionals, to pursue a PhD and a research-focused career. Given these developments, it might not be surprising if the discussion sections of journal articles have become a place as devoted to justifying and recommending

New Directions for Student Services, no. 147, Fall 2014 © 2014 Wiley Periodicals, Inc.
Published online in Wiley Online Library (wileyonlinelibrary.com) • DOI: 10.1002/ss.20095

future, more sophisticated studies as to detailing thorough, thoughtful implications for practice.

So, as calls for student affairs professionals to use research to inform their practice have escalated, the relevant research has become more difficult to understand. Our goal in this volume of *New Directions for Student Services* is to draw implications for practice from the findings of the Wabash National Study of Liberal Arts Education, an investigation that followed thousands of college students at over 50 colleges and universities and has resulted in numerous journal articles. In Chapter 1, we, along with James P. Barber, conceptualize research-driven practice and offer an overview of the methods used in the Wabash National Study, the backdrop for this volume. In Chapter 2, Tricia A. Seifert discusses the development of moral character in college, including educational experiences that influence moral development. In Chapter 3, Michael S. Hevel and Daniel A. Bureau explore research-driven practice in fraternity/sorority life by synthesizing the research in this area. In Chapter 4, Kathleen M. Goodman and Nicholas A. Bowman discuss diversity on college campuses and identify policies and practices to influence student learning along diversity-related outcomes. In Chapter 5, Georgianna L. Martin and Melandie McGee explore the direct effects of student affairs professionals on college student development, an often missing piece from the student affairs literature. In Chapter 6, James P. Barber considers how students integrate their learning over four years of college using findings from the qualitative side of the Wabash National Study. In Chapter 7, Teniell L. Trolian synthesizes the findings from the Wabash National Study on a variety of "at-risk" student populations and discusses the role of student affairs professionals in improving college outcomes for all students. Finally, in Chapter 8, V. Leilani Kupo reflects on what it means to be a scholar-practitioner in student affairs today.

Georgianna L. Martin
Michael S. Hevel
Editors

GEORGIANNA L. MARTIN *is an assistant professor of higher education and student affairs at the University of Southern Mississippi.*

MICHAEL S. HEVEL *is an assistant professor of higher education at the University of Arkansas.*

NEW DIRECTIONS FOR STUDENT SERVICES • DOI: 10.1002/ss

1

This chapter explores the concept of research-driven practice in student affairs and provides an overview of the Wabash National Study of Liberal Arts Education.

Conceptualizing Research-Driven Practice and the Wabash National Study

Georgianna L. Martin, Michael S. Hevel, James P. Barber

Early morning staff meetings. Parent phone calls. One-on-one advising meetings with student leaders. Student conduct meetings. Developing learning outcomes. Responding to campus crises. Trudging through email messages. Late-night student organization meetings. The day-to-day work of a student affairs professional is personally rewarding and critical to student success, but it is often high stress and fast-paced. Racing to put out fires during long workdays with little time to plan for the next week or month, let alone keep up with the latest research in the field, becomes commonplace for many professionals. The primary goal of this volume is to demonstrate practical ways student affairs professionals can use research to elevate their work with students. We use findings from the Wabash National Study of Liberal Arts Education (WNS) as a backdrop to accomplish this goal. This chapter lays the groundwork for the subsequent chapters in this volume. In this chapter, we first explore research-driven practice as a professional imperative. Next, we provide a conceptual overview of the WNS followed by an abbreviated review of both the quantitative and qualitative methods used in this large-scale, longitudinal study.

Defining Research-Driven Practice

The concept of research-driven practice is at the core of this volume. Conceptually, research-driven practice is intentionally more holistic than the *data-driven decision making* more commonly referred to in education circles. Employed frequently in K–12 education as a response to state and federal accountability requirements, data-driven decision making uses assessment

The research for this volume was supported by a generous grant from the Center of Inquiry in the Liberal Arts at Wabash College to the Center for Research on Undergraduate Education at The University of Iowa.

NEW DIRECTIONS FOR STUDENT SERVICES, no. 147, Fall 2014 © 2014 Wiley Periodicals, Inc.
Published online in Wiley Online Library (wileyonlinelibrary.com) • DOI: 10.1002/ss.20096

results and institutional research to make more informed decisions. Marsh, Pane, and Hamilton (2006) define data-driven decision making in education as:

> teachers, principals, and administrators systematically collecting and analyzing various types of data, including input, process, outcome and satisfaction data, to guide a range of decisions to help improve the success of students and schools. Achievement test data, in particular, play a prominent role in federal and state accountability policies. (p. 1)

By contrast, research-driven practice is a broader approach, differing from data-driven decision making in two main ways: (a) attention to the entire research process, including the motivating research questions, participant selection, methodology, and limitations in addition to the findings; and (b) a focus on comprehensive practice, including student mentoring, programmatic design, and student learning support, rather than an emphasis on the decision-making process.

Some scholars have phrased this mode of being by using the terms "scholar-practitioner" or "practitioner-scholar" to acknowledge the confluence of theory and research with practical application (e.g., Carpenter & Stimpson, 2007; Erwin & Wise, 2002; Sriram & Oster, 2012). For example, Carpenter (2001) outlined the elements of scholarly practice as being intentional, grounded in theory/research/data, peer-reviewed, accepting of a variety of perspectives, collaborative, open to change, unselfish, careful, regenerative, and contextual.

Still others suggest a more complex way of viewing the spaces student affairs educators occupy with respect to the scholarship in the field. Manning pondered the division between faculty and practitioners in student affairs by proposing a continuum from pure scholar to pure practitioner, arguing that not all educators in student affairs should contribute to the creation of scholarship (Jablonski, Mena, Manning, Carpenter, & Siko, 2006). In her model, there are *pure scholars*, individuals who have exclusively contributed to the scholarship in the field and who have spent little time as administrators. The next point along her continuum is the *scholar/practitioner*. This refers to someone who has previously served as an administrator, but who currently occupies a faculty or research-related role. The scholarship of the scholar/practitioner, Manning suggested, is a combination of empirical research and reflective writing about student affairs practice. In contrast, she titles the next group the *practitioner/scholars*. These are full-time professionals and administrators who write and make scholarly contributions to the field in addition to their professional practice in student affairs. Manning's next group, the *practitioners,* are those full-time professionals who are not actively contributing to the scholarship in the field, but who consistently use theory and research in their practice. The final group along this continuum is what Manning calls the *pure practitioners*. These are individuals who place little value on the use of scholarship to inform practice. Manning's framework serves to move educators out of an either/or mode of thinking about the role of scholarship in our field and serves as a valuable tool for conceptualizing the diversity of roles among professionals and scholars.

In this volume, we emphasize the middle three modes of operating (scholar/practitioners, practitioner/scholars, and practitioners), as each of these frames offers at least some integration of theory, research, and practice. We believe these middle modes work toward Carpenter's (2001) conceptualization of scholarly practice and thus further the professionalization and the credibility of all student affairs educators. In this volume, we employ findings from the Wabash National Study of Liberal Arts Education to illustrate the ways in which student affairs professionals in higher education can use research to enhance their practice.

Overview of the Wabash National Study

The Wabash National Study of Liberal Arts Education (WNS) was a national, concurrent mixed method in design, longitudinal study that explores the college experiences that influence students' development along key educational outcomes over four years of college. The two primary goals of the WNS were to understand the teaching practices, activities, and environmental structures that fostered a liberal arts education and to create tools to assess liberal arts education in American colleges and universities (Wabash National Study, n.d.). In particular, the WNS focused on developmental outcomes associated with a liberal arts education, including self-authorship and seven liberal arts outcomes: integration of learning, inclination to inquire and lifelong learning, effective reasoning and problem solving, moral character, intercultural effectiveness, leadership, and psychological well-being (King, Kendall Brown, Lindsay, & VanHecke, 2007). These liberal arts educational outcomes are distinctive from other types of learning outcomes because of their holistic nature and the connection between outcomes that incorporate cognitive, interpersonal, and intrapersonal development. The WNS sought to explore these seven outcomes. Although all seven outcomes were explored in the qualitative branch of the WNS, only six outcomes were measured in the quantitative branch of the study. Integration of learning was only studied in the qualitative portion of the study. In the sections that follow, we offer brief overviews of the quantitative and qualitative methods used in the WNS to provide context for the remaining chapters in this volume.

Quantitative Methods in the WNS.   The quantitative data presented in this volume largely represent the student sample from 17 four-year institutions that entered the WNS during the fall of 2006. However, two additional cohorts of institutions and students began the study in 2007 and 2008, respectively. Although most of the published findings from the WNS

NEW DIRECTIONS FOR STUDENT SERVICES • DOI: 10.1002/ss

only use findings from the 2006 entering cohort, occasionally authors chose to include multiple cohorts in their analyses.

Institutional and Student Sample. Researchers used a two-step sampling strategy to select institutions for the WNS. First, 19 institutions were selected from over 60 colleges and universities that responded to a national invitation to participate in the WNS. Institutions were chosen based on their vision of liberal arts education, as well as to reflect a variety of characteristics, including institutional type (e.g., liberal arts college, research university, regional university) and control (public or private), size, and location, among others. The sample in the study consisted of incoming first-year students at 17 four-year colleges and universities and 2 two-year colleges from the Northeast/Middle-Atlantic, Southeast, Midwest, and Pacific Coast regions in the United States. Using the 2007 Carnegie Classification of Institutions, 3 of the participating institutions were research extensive universities, 3 were comprehensive regional universities that did not grant the doctorate, 11 were baccalaureate liberal arts colleges, and 2 two-year colleges.

The individuals in the sample were first-year, full-time, undergraduate students at these institutions. In the fall of 2006, the sample was selected in one of three ways. First, at the largest participating institution in the study, the sample was selected randomly from the incoming class in the College of Arts and Sciences. For the remaining larger institutions, the sample was selected randomly from the incoming first-year class. Third, for a number of the smallest institutions in the study—all liberal arts colleges—the sample was the entire incoming first-year class. Students were invited to participate in a national longitudinal study examining how a college education affects students, with the ultimate goal of improving the undergraduate experience.

The initial data collection occurred in fall 2006, with 4,193 students from the 17 four-year institutions. This first data collection lasted between 90 and 100 minutes, and students were paid a stipend of $50 for their participation. Data collected included a WNS precollege survey that sought information on student demographic characteristics, high school experiences, life/career plans, and family background. Students also completed a series of instruments that measured dimensions of cognitive and personal development theoretically associated with a liberal arts education, such as critical thinking, moral reasoning, need for cognition, inclination to inquire and lifelong learning, and psychological well-being (King et al., 2007).

Two follow-up data collections occurred, once in the spring of 2007 (approximately at the end of the first year of college) and once in the spring of 2010 (approximately at the end of the fourth year of college). Each of these data collections took about two hours and participating students were paid an additional stipend of $50 each time. Both follow-up collections included gathering two types of data: information on students' college experiences using the National Survey of Student Engagement (NSSE) and the WNS Student Experiences Survey, and posttest data using the series of instruments measuring aspects of students' intellectual and personal development. The entire data collection was administered and conducted by ACT, Inc. (formerly the American College Testing Program).

Of the original sample of 4,193 students who participated in the initial fall 2006 data collection, 2,212 participated in the spring 2010 follow-up, for a response rate of 52.8%. These students represented approximately 10% of the total population of incoming first-year students at the 17 participating institutions. Researchers developed weighting algorithms to provide some adjustment for potential response bias by sex, race, academic ability, and institution in the samples analyzed.

The primary dependent measures in the WNS included the following instruments: the critical thinking portion of the Collegiate Assessment of Academic Proficiency (CAAP) to assess effective reasoning and problem solving (ACT, 1991); the Defining Issues Test 2 to assess moral reasoning (Rest, Narvaez, Thoma, & Bebeau, 1999); the Need for Cognition Scale (Cacioppo, Petty, Feinstein, & Jarvis, 1996) and the Positive Attitude Toward Literacy Scale (Bray, Pascarella, & Pierson, 2004) to assess the inclination to inquire and lifelong learning; the Miville-Guzman Universality-Diversity Scale (Miville et al., 1999) and the Openness to Diversity/Challenge Scale (Pascarella, Edison, Nora, Hagedorn, & Terenzini, 1996) to assess intercultural effectiveness; the Ryff Scales of Psychological Well-Being (Ryff & Keyes, 1995) to assess well-being; and the revised version II of the Socially Responsible Leadership Scale (Tyree, 1998) to measure leadership. Each of these dependent measures was carefully selected by the principal investigators of the WNS in the years leading up to the initial data collection. Complete descriptions, coding, reliability, and validity information of all dependent and independent measures used in the study can be found in the quantitative research methods report for the WNS (Pascarella, 2007).

Qualitative Methods in the WNS.   The qualitative branch of the research team selected 6 institutions from the 19 institutions in the WNS to participate in the interview phase of the study. Institutional type, geographic location, and diversity of student body were all considered in the selection process. The selected institutions included four small liberal arts colleges, one mid-sized and one large university, two Hispanic-serving institutions, and one that enrolls approximately 50% African-American and 50% White students.

Researchers selected interview participants from students at the six institutions who completed the quantitative survey component of the study and indicated their willingness to participate in an interview, oversampling men and Students of Color to yield a more balanced distribution. The study team interviewed 315 students early in the fall of 2006 (hereafter Year 1). About one third of these students identified as African American, Hispanic, or as Asian/Pacific Islanders; the remainder identified as White. About 10% were born in countries other than the United States. The sample was 54% female. Researchers were able to contact and reinterview 228 of these students in fall 2007 (Year 2), 204 in fall 2008 (Year 3), and 177 in fall 2009 (Year 4).

Trained interviewers conducted individual interviews that lasted 60 to 90 minutes; these were audio recorded and transcribed verbatim. Participants received a $30 stipend per interview. The interview was organized into three segments to give respondents maximum freedom to identify relevant content yet elicit information about the practices and conditions that fostered growth on the seven outcomes and self-authorship (Baxter Magolda & King, 2007). The opening segment focused on how students' entering characteristics (i.e., ways of constructing knowledge, self, relationships; personal history) affected achievement of or development toward self-authorship. The second (and primary) segment of the interview explored the educational experiences students saw as most significant and how they made meaning of these experiences. The third segment addressed the students' synthesis of their experiences and patterns in their meaning making.

Working from the complete interview transcripts, trained research team members created summaries of each interview comprised of three major elements: (a) overview of the student's background characteristics; (b) description of each experience the student identified as important, its effect on the student (i.e., what the student learned from the experience), and illustrative quotes from the student; and (c) assessment of the student's developmental meaning making in cognitive, intrapersonal, and interpersonal domains, as well as an overall assessment across dimensions illustrated with student quotes (Baxter Magolda & King, 2012).

To guide self-authorship assessment, team members used a 10-position continuum (Baxter Magolda & King, 2012). This continuum reflects the gradual movement of external frameworks to the background and the internal voice to the foreground. This process mirrors Perry's (1970) description of the evolution of his developmental positions. Researchers embraced his use of the term *position* because it reflects the particular structure a person uses to understand knowledge, identity, and relationships at a particular point in time. This 10-position continuum reflects a nominal scale, as is the case with Perry's nine positions. Each position reflects a more complex meaning-making structure than the prior position; however this is not a lock-step stage model. The positions evolve gradually, vary in duration, and movement on the continuum is better characterized as a helix than a line.

Determining the developmental effect of each experience was important for understanding factors that affect students' development. Researchers followed the approach introduced by King, Baxter Magolda, Barber, Kendall Brown, and Lindsay (2009) to identify those cases where a student reported that as a result of an experience, she or he now used a more complex approach to understanding knowledge, oneself, or relationships.

King et al. (2009) termed these "developmentally effective experiences" (DEEs) to reflect their positive developmental impact.

In the qualitative branch of the WNS, researchers addressed issues of trustworthiness and quality in several ways. Extensive training for all interviewers and summarizers included training in the constructivist-developmental foundation that guided the interview construction and analysis, training in the purpose of the interview, practice interviewing with feedback, an analysis of interviewer subjectivities, and practice summary writing with feedback. (Additional details on the training process can be found in Baxter Magolda & King, 2012.)

The sheer size of the interview sample (924 interviews) prohibited using the traditional approaches to trustworthiness (e.g., member checking) due to funding considerations and logistical difficulties (the in-person contact was limited to the annual interview weeks on each campus). Instead, researchers implemented a rigorous process to establish the credibility of the interview analysis. The process for establishing trustworthiness of the developmental assessments evolved as the assessment system became more complex. Over time, researchers expanded and refined their understanding of the assessment through pooled judgment rather than relying on individual assessments. The principal investigators continued to review approximately three summaries from each new summarizer throughout the course of the study; they also reviewed experienced summarizers' work upon request.

Credibility was enhanced through extended engagement with the students; individual interviews took place annually and typically lasted over an hour. Rapport building was built into the first part of the interview so that participants would be comfortable with the interview process; researchers attempted to use the same interviewer in subsequent interviews for continuity. Additionally, students had the opportunity to provide feedback about the interview process at the end of each interview. Participants were offered copies of the verbatim transcripts and invited to fill in words that were inaudible, correct factual errors, and offer comments or additional insights to a team member after receiving the transcript. Transferability was heightened through the use of thick description of the narratives whenever possible.

Using the WNS Findings to Inform Practice

The magnitude of its scope, rigor, and intentional research design situates the WNS to offer important insights into a variety of college student experiences and student affairs programs and services. A simple glance at the list of publications in major higher education journals and presentations at research, policy, and practice-oriented national conferences using data from the WNS over the past seven years suggests that this national study is already influencing what educators understand about college experiences today (Center for Research on Undergraduate Education, n.d.; Pascarella &

Blaich, 2013). To date, much of the national buzz around the WNS has been related to findings on practices inside the classroom on college campuses (e.g., Berrett, 2012; Pascarella, Blaich, Martin, & Hanson, 2011; Schmidt, 2011). Less attention has been given to the WNS in student affairs circles even though many of the studies have direct implications for educators' work with students outside of the classroom.

In the remaining chapters of this volume, studies employing data from the WNS with implications for student affairs professionals are presented in order to spark dialogue about the ways in which these data might improve policy and practice in student affairs administration in the coming years. As we reflect on the widening divide between researchers and practitioners in student affairs and the philosophical charge to allow research, at least in part, to drive practice, it is our hope that the chapters contained within this volume will serve as a framework for how professionals might synthesize, critically analyze, and apply research to their own practice in student affairs.

References

American College Testing Program (ACT). (1991). *CAAP technical handbook.* Iowa City, IA: Author.

Baxter Magolda, M. B., & King, P. M. (2007). Constructing conversations to assess meaning-making: Self-authorship interviews. *Journal of College Student Development, 48*(5), 491–508. doi:10.1353/csd.2007.0055

Baxter Magolda, M. B., & King, P. M. (2012). *Assessing meaning making and self-authorship: Theory, research, and application* [ASHE Higher Education Report Series, 38(3)]. San Francisco, CA: Jossey-Bass. doi:10.1002/aehe.20003

Berrett, D. (2012, November 19). Encounters with diversity, on campus and in course-work, bolster critical thinking skills. *The Chronicle of Higher Education.* Retrieved from http://chronicle.com/article/Diversity-Bolsters/135858/

Bray, G. B., Pascarella, E. T., & Pierson, C. T. (2004). Postsecondary education and some dimensions of literacy development. An exploration of longitudinal evidence. *Reading Research Quarterly, 39*, 306–330.

Cacioppo, J., Petty, R., Feinstein, J., & Jarvis, W. (1996). Dispositional differences in cognitive motivation: The life of individuals differing in need for cognition. *Psychological Bulletin, 119*, 197–253.

Carpenter, S. (2001). Student affairs scholarship (re?) considered: Toward a scholarship of practice. *Journal of College Student Development, 42*(4), 301–318.

Carpenter, S., & Stimpson, M. T. (2007). Professionalism, scholarly practice, and professional development in student affairs. *NASPA Journal, 44*(2), 265–284.

Center for Research on Undergraduate Education. (n.d.). *Leaders. Scholars. Innovators.* The University of Iowa, College of Education. Retrieved from http://www.education.uiowa.edu/centers/crue/publications

Erwin, T. D., & Wise, S. L. (2002). A scholar-practitioner model for assessment. In T. W. Banta & Associates (Eds.), *Building a scholarship of assessment* (pp. 67–81). San Francisco, CA: Jossey-Bass.

Jablonski, M. A., Mena, S. B., Manning, K., Carpenter, S., & Siko, K. L. (2006). Scholarship in student affairs revisited: The summit on scholarship, March 2006. *NASPA Journal, 43*(4), 182–200.

King, P. M., Baxter Magolda, M. B., Barber, J. P., Kendall Brown, M., & Lindsay, N. K. (2009). Developmentally effective experiences for promoting self-authorship. *Mind, Brain, and Education, 3*(2), 106–116. doi:10.1111/j.1751-228X.2009.01061.x

King, P. M., Kendall Brown, M., Lindsay, N. K., & VanHecke, J. R. (2007). Liberal arts student learning outcomes: An integrated perspective. *About Campus, 12*(4), 2–9. doi:10.1002/abc.222

Marsh, J. A., Pane, J. F., & Hamilton, L. S. (2006). *Making sense of data-driven decision making in education: Evidence from recent RAND research.* Retrieved from http://www.rand.org/content/dam/rand/pubs/occasional_papers/2006/RAND_OP170.pdf

Miville, M., Gelso, C., Pannu, R., Liu, W., Touradji, P., Holloway, P., & Fuertes, J. (1999). Appreciating similarities and valuing differences: The Miville-Guzman Universality-Diversity Scale. *Journal of Counseling Psychology, 46*(3), 291–307.

Pascarella, E. T. (2007). *Methodological report for Wabash National Study of Liberal Arts Education.* Iowa City, IA: Center for Research on Undergraduate Education.

Pascarella, E. T., & Blaich, C. (2013). Lessons from the Wabash National Study of Liberal Arts Education. *Change, 45*(2), 6–15. doi:10.1080/00091383.2013.764257

Pascarella, E. T., Blaich, C., Martin, G. L., & Hanson, J. M. (2011). How robust are the findings of *Academically Adrift?* Evidence from the Wabash National Study. *Change, 43*(3), 20–22.

Pascarella, E. T., Edison, M., Nora, A., Hagedorn, L., & Terenzini, P. (1996). Influences on students' openness to diversity and challenge in the first year of college. *Journal of Higher Education, 67*(2), 174–195.

Perry, W. G. (1970). *Forms of intellectual and ethical development in the college years: A scheme.* New York, NY: Holt, Rinehart, and Winston.

Rest, J., Narvaez, D., Thoma, S., & Bebeau, M. (1999). DIT2: Devising and testing a revised instrument of moral judgment. *Journal of Educational Psychology, 91,* 644–659.

Ryff, C., & Keyes, C. (1995). The structure of psychological well-being revisited. *Journal of Personality and Social Psychology, 69,* 719–727.

Schmidt, P. (2011, April 11). Study finds a big gap between college seniors' real and perceived learning. *The Chronicle of Higher Education.* Retrieved from http://chronicle.com/article/Study-Finds-a-Big-Gap-Between/127087/

Sriram, R., & Oster, M. (2012). Reclaiming the "scholar" in scholar-practitioner. *Journal of Student Affairs Research and Practice, 49*(4), 377–396.

Tyree, T. (1998). *Designing an instrument to measure socially responsible leadership using the social change model of leadership development* (Unpublished doctoral dissertation). University of Maryland-College Park, College Park.

Wabash National Study. (n.d.). *Center of Inquiry in the Liberal Arts and Wabash College.* Retrieved from http://www.liberalarts.wabash.edu/study-overview/

GEORGIANNA L. MARTIN *is an assistant professor of higher education and student affairs at the University of Southern Mississippi.*

MICHAEL S. HEVEL *is an assistant professor of higher education at the University of Arkansas.*

JAMES P. BARBER *is an assistant professor of education at the College of William & Mary.*

2

This chapter synthesizes WNS research that examined moral character and concludes with recommendations for student affairs practice.

Developing Moral Character

Tricia A. Seifert

How do students decide whether or not to cheat on a test? How do they determine whether they will use a fake ID to get into a bar? Students face these questions and many others during college. But how do they resolve their course of action in handling moral and ethical dilemmas and how are students' college experiences facilitating their moral reasoning and development of a personal code of ethics? Scandals highlighting lapses in personal integrity and willful disregard for collective responsibility appear in the media regularly. Within this context, external stakeholder organizations have called on higher education institutions to view students' moral and ethical development as not simply an option but part of the "standard equipment of our graduates" (Kellogg Commission on the Future of State Land Grant Universities, 1997, p. 27). Given that liberal arts education is intended to cultivate students' integrity, sense of collective responsibility, passion, balance, and vision (Thomas, 2002) as necessary dispositions for wise and ethical stewardship, it follows that moral character, defined as the capacity to make and act on moral or ethical judgments and treat others with fairness and compassion (King, Kendall Brown, Lindsay, & VanHecke, 2007), was part of the integrated framework of liberal arts outcomes included in the WNS.

The purpose of this chapter is to synthesize the WNS research that examined moral character as an outcome. This chapter focuses on the relationships between measures of moral character and student demographic and background characteristics, institutional context, course content, and curricular and cocurricular conditions of the student experience. Responding to King and colleagues' (2007) suggestion that a campus-wide approach is needed to develop the interdependent outcomes of a liberal arts education in which wise and ethical stewardship is the overarching aim, the chapter concludes with recommendations of how findings from the WNS research can inform student affairs practice.

The outcome, moral character, was operationalized quantitatively in the WNS in two ways. First, the Defining Issues Test, 2 (DIT2; Rest,

New Directions for Student Services, no. 147, Fall 2014 © 2014 Wiley Periodicals, Inc.
Published online in Wiley Online Library (wileyonlinelibrary.com) • DOI: 10.1002/ss.20097

Narvaez, Thoma, & Bebeau, 1999) measured the degree to which students use principles to guide their decision making when faced with a moral dilemma. Most of the WNS studies that examined moral reasoning (e.g., Mayhew, 2012; Mayhew, Seifert, & Pascarella, 2010; Mayhew, Seifert, Pascarella, Nelson Laird, & Blaich, 2012b) used the composite N2 score, which is comprised of two parts: (a) the degree to which respondents prioritize items from a societal perspective, where fairness serves larger communities, including strangers (postconventional) as opposed to a system in which fairness serves oneself (preconventional) or one's close friends and family (conventional); and (b) the degree to which respondents reject simplistic or biased solutions (Bebeau & Thoma, 2003). Higher N2 scores reflect an individual's capacity for reasoning about moral issues grounded in a system of fairness that serves the public good (consistent with Thomas's assertion of ethical stewardship); lower N2 scores tend to reflect reasoning about moral issues from a fairness perspective that is self-serving. Moral character was also measured by asking students to self-assess their growth in developing a personal code of ethics. Finally, some participants from the interview portion of the WNS study shared moral dilemmas they faced and how they worked through these dilemmas.

Review of the Literature

No fewer than 12 research articles and presentations from the WNS have examined moral character as an outcome. In some cases, the articles investigated the influence of a host of curricular or cocurricular experiences on the entire integrated liberal arts outcome framework of which moral character was one outcome (e.g., Seifert et al., 2008), and in other cases, the articles focused on the curricular and cocurricular conditions associated with moral reasoning development as the sole outcome of interest (e.g., Mayhew et al., 2010). Together, this body of research has examined the relationships between student demographic and background characteristics, context, course content, curricular and cocurricular conditions of the student experience, students' values and meaning-making orientations, and moral character. The next section summarizes the findings from the WNS research examining moral character as a liberal arts outcome.

Student Demographic and Background Characteristics

Consistent with past research (for a thorough review, see King & Mayhew, 2002), research from the WNS found that demographic and students' background characteristics are significantly related to differences in moral reasoning development. Women, students who had higher levels of tested academic preparation (ACT score or equivalent), as well as those who reported greater precollege cognitive motivation (operationalized using the Need for Cognition Scale), experienced greater gains in moral reasoning at the end of the first year of college (Lindsay, Barnhardt, DeGraw, King, & Baxter Magolda, 2007; Mayhew, 2012; Mayhew et al., 2010, 2012a). No differences were found in students' moral reasoning development by level of parental education (Mayhew et al., 2012a; Padgett, Johnson, & Pascarella, 2012), and the small statistically significant bivariate difference found by year in college—a proxy for age in which first- and second-year students were compared to third- and fourth-year students—was reduced to non-significance in the presence of other variables (Lindsay et al., 2007).

Few WNS studies found differences in moral reasoning development by race/ethnicity (Lindsay et al., 2007; Mayhew et al., 2010, 2012a; Padgett et al., 2012). However, in the only multilevel investigation of moral reasoning, controlling for a host of student-level variables, Mayhew (2012) found African-American students were less likely to gain in their moral reasoning compared to their White peers over the course of the first year of college.

A small body of research has examined the influence of student demographic and background characteristics on students' ability to self-assess their gains in moral character. Bowman (2010a, 2010b) examined the single item in which students self-assess their gains on developing a "personal code of ethics" and correlated this with students' objectively assessed N2 moral reasoning score. To the extent that institutional researchers and other education policymakers employ self-reported measures to approximate student growth, one should exercise caution.

There are nontrivial concerns regarding the validity of such self-reported measures as proxies for objectively measured forms of development (Bowman, 2010b). In addition to the validity concern, Bowman (2010a) found demographic and background characteristics appear to influence students' efficacy to identify moral growth. Although students with different high school GPAs did not differ in their ability to self-assess gains in moral development (in other words, the correlations between the objective and subjective assessments did not differ significantly by high school GPA group), the magnitude of the correlation between the objective and subjective measures of moral development was more strongly positive for first-generation students than their non-first-generation peers. This suggests first-generation students are more accurate in their self-assessment of their growth in moral character than their non-first-generation peers. Although correlations between students' objective and subjective assessments did not differ between Asian/Pacific Islander, Latino, and White students, there was a negative correlation between the objective and subjective assessments of moral development for African-American students. Said another way, African-American students were significantly worse in estimating their gains in moral character development than their White peers.

Since few WNS studies have found consistent differences in the moral character outcome between students from different racial/ethnic groups, caution should be used in extrapolating from the two studies that found such differences (Bowman, 2010a; Mayhew, 2012). Synthesizing the WNS findings as they examine the relationship between demographic and background characteristics and moral reasoning, there appears to be an opportunity for educators to consider how they develop environments to encourage moral growth and the ability to self-assess that growth for all students but particularly for men, African-American students, and students who come to college with lower levels of academic preparation and motivation to engage in cognitively effortful activities.

Context

Three studies examined the relationship between institutional context and students' moral reasoning development. Mayhew (2012) examined the extent to which students' moral reasoning development differed by institutional type. Controlling for a host of student-level characteristics, students at community colleges had lower moral reasoning scores at the end of the first year of college than their peers at liberal arts colleges. Although the differences in gains in moral reasoning between students at liberal arts colleges and their peers at regional universities approached statistical significance ($p < .10$), no difference was found in moral reasoning between students at liberal arts colleges and research universities.

Institutional type is not something institutions are in a position to alter generally. However, researchers may approximate institutional context by averaging students' experiences at an institution and examining how the resulting proxy of institutional context relates to student outcomes. The only study that examined institutions as the level of analysis averaged student responses on the National Survey of Student Engagement benchmarks to investigate the relationship between these and the institution's average moral reasoning score (Pascarella, Seifert, & Blaich, 2010). Controlling for institutional averaged precollege moral reasoning, only the enriching educational experiences had a positive relationship with moral reasoning at the end of the first year of college; none of the other average benchmark scores were related to moral reasoning development at the institutional level.

One may critique that students do not experience the average level of their institution's enriching educational experiences, academic challenge, active and collaborative learning, student–faculty interaction, or supportive campus environment. Students experience these conditions as individuals but rarely in the discrete fashion characteristic of the five NSSE benchmarks. In an effort to measure the seamlessness of a student's higher education experience, Seifert and colleagues (2008) created a composite measure of "liberal arts experiences" to examine its relationship to a host of liberal arts outcomes. In the four-institution cross-sectional pilot study that preceded the larger longitudinal WNS study, controlling for a host of background characteristics, they found no relationship between students' reports of liberal arts experiences and moral reasoning in the pilot sample from the WNS study.

King (2009) asserted that moral "development occurs in context, in interaction with the environment" (p. 613). However, the three studies examining the relationship between institutional context and moral development may have been too distant from the actual environment(s) in which higher education administrators and faculty facilitate students' moral reasoning. Other research from the WNS study has focused specifically on the relationship between types of coursework and conditions students experience in and out of the classroom with moral reasoning development. Findings from these studies provide clearer avenues from which educators can examine and alter their practice in order to best foster students' moral development.

Content

Several studies examined the relationship between aggregate patterns of coursework completed, defined either as number of liberal arts courses taken or number of courses taken in the STEM and health fields. To be clear, most of this research used aggregate coursework patterns as a control measure. However, in moving from distant measures of institutional context to the content of the environments in which college and university administrators and faculty may facilitate students' moral reasoning development, findings related to coursework patterns are illustrative. Mayhew et al. (2010) found no relationship between liberal arts coursework and moral reasoning at the end of the first year of college, although Padgett et al. (2012), using a different subsample and set of predictors in the regression model, found a very small negative relationship between liberal arts coursework and moral reasoning.

Turning to a different cluster of disciplines, the number of courses taken in the STEM and health fields had a negative relationship with students' moral reasoning development (Mayhew et al., 2012a). One could argue it is hard to reform curricula to better facilitate moral growth based on the number of courses students have taken across such diverse disciplinary areas, like the traditional arts and sciences or STEM and health disciplines. Another set of studies provide more insight into potential ways to create learning environments by focusing directly at the relationship between course content and moral reasoning development.

Most of the studies that examined course content investigated the relationship between students' encounters and engagement with diversity issues and moral reasoning development. Mayhew et al. (2010) found the number of diversity courses a student had taken had no relationship with their end-of-first-year moral reasoning development. This was consistent with Bowman's (2009) findings regarding the general effects of diversity courses on moral reasoning development. However, Bowman probed a bit deeper by examining the conditional effects of diversity courses and students' socioeconomic status on moral reasoning development. There was a positive effect for taking two or more diversity courses for students from high-income families on moral reasoning. Yet, in subgroup analysis, this effect was not statistically significant although students from low- to middle-income families who took three or more diversity courses had greater gains in moral reasoning than their low- to middle-income peers who did not take any diversity courses. Whether it is simply going on study abroad (Salisbury, 2011) or taking courses that focus on diverse cultures or perspectives, the weight of these findings suggests the content of the experience or course alone does not seem to be sufficient to stimulate moral growth. Another set of articles examined the curricular and cocurricular conditions that facilitated moral development.

Conditions

It seems that substantively engaging with, reflecting on, and integrating perspectives different from one's own are necessary to stimulate moral growth. Although Mayhew et al. (2010) found no relationship with courses in which students were asked to connect course material to career and society, courses that asked students to connect historical, political, and social events were related to students' moral reasoning development. This notion of connection was furthered in the analysis by Mayhew et al. (2012b) in which they found a small positive relationship with a composite measure of deep learning (summed scores on the NSSE higher order thinking, reflective thinking, and integrative thinking subscales). However, in a subscale analysis, integrative learning was the subscale in which the relationship with moral reasoning development was the strongest. These findings support the perspective offered by Nancy Thomas in which she articulates "a quality liberal education leads students to reflect on their place in the world and locate themselves historically and socially" (Thomas, 2002, p. 30, quoted in King et al., 2007, p. 3).

These studies suggest the influence educators have in creating learning environments that facilitate moral growth. Several studies examined the conditions students experienced in and out of the classroom. Academic challenge and high expectations (Mayhew et al., 2010; Padgett et al., 2012), good teaching and high-quality interactions with faculty (Mayhew et al., 2010), as well as influential peer interactions (Mayhew et al., 2010) all positively contributed to moral reasoning development in the first year of college. Research from the WNS suggests that educators are drawing from Nevitt Sanford's principle of challenge and support, in which the two must be balanced. According to King (2009), "when support is too high, there is no perceived need to change one's outlook or find a more adaptive stance. When challenge is too high, it is common to feel overwhelmed and tempted to give up and not stay engaged with the problem at hand" (p. 614).

Recognizing Developmental Phases

The principle of challenge and support is keenly related to students' developmental phase (King, 2009). Rest et al. (1999) detail the existence of two phases associated with each stage of moral reasoning: consolidated and transitional. In the consolidated phase, individuals use preexisting, context-independent mental models of reasoning when interacting with people and events. In the transitional phase, individuals draw from a variety of situational environmental cues, appear to be more open to suggestion, and willing to change their perspective. One could extrapolate that individuals in transitional phases of moral reasoning are more open to face and resolve the dissonance and disequilibrium that is a necessary condition of development.

Research from the WNS found statistically significant relationships between curricular and cocurricular conditions and moral reasoning development for students in a transitional phase of moral reasoning, but these relationships were not significant for students in a consolidated phase (Mayhew, et al., 2012b). For example, influential peer interactions, number of courses that asked students to connect historical, political, and social events, as well as the number of diversity courses were all positively associated with moral reasoning development at the end of the first year of college for students in a transitional phase of moral reasoning but had no effect for students in a consolidated phase.

Lindsay and colleagues (2007) also found students' sense of openness and interest in encountering diverse perspectives, whether socially or in courses, and developing a meaningful philosophy of life contributed positively to moral reasoning development. Curiously, valuing the importance of helping others as well as success in one's own business each had unique negative associations with moral reasoning development. They also found that students who had a more internally defined meaning-making structure had greater moral reasoning development than their peers whose meaning-making structure was externally defined (e.g., maintaining the morals from their upbringing).

These two studies, in their own unique ways, examined students' openness to engaging the dissonance and disequilibrium often experienced in the first year of college. What is interesting is that the measures of challenge and support in the Mayhew and colleagues (2012b) study (academic challenge and high expectations, and good teaching and high-quality interactions with faculty) were not significant predictors of moral reasoning development for students in either the transitional or consolidated phases but students' meaning-making structures were clearly related to moral reasoning development. Given that past research has suggested the importance of challenge and support in developing learning partnerships to facilitate self-authorship (Baxter Magolda & King, 2004), an opportunity appears for student affairs practitioners to challenge and support students in transitional and consolidated phases "by concentrating on the fundamental meaning making orientation of students and utilizing a range of contexts and experiences" (Lindsay et al., 2007, p. 30).

The body of evidence from the WNS suggests that moral character development in the first year of college differs by student demographic and background characteristics and that various curricular and cocurricular conditions provide fruitful avenues for student affairs practitioners to be part of a campus-wide approach to facilitate moral development. In the concluding section, I synthesize the implications for practice from the reviewed studies and make targeted recommendations for student affairs practice.

Discussion

The body of research reviewed in this chapter suggests that moral character development is a process that students engage in different ways and at different times. To that end, developing personal integrity and sense of collective responsibility—two of the key dispositions of wise and ethical stewardship—require students to embark on a developmental journey. The role of higher education, then, is to encourage students to take the first step out the door, and if already departed, continue their journey. Women as well as students who are more academically prepared, motivated to engage in cognitively demanding activities, and open to and interested in different perspectives (likely those who are in the transitional phase of their moral reasoning stage) appear to be developmentally ready for their journey upon matriculation while other students seem to need an opportunity to consider their moral positions at multiple points within their college career. Considering that the development of character, conscience, and individual and social responsibility "should be part of the standard equipment of our graduates, not options" (Kellogg Commission on the Future of State Land Grant Universities, 1997, p. 27), what can student affairs practitioners do to foster moral and ethical development in all students with whom they interact? It seems that student affairs practitioners who educate for transformational learning are best up to the task.

In his landmark book *Learning as Transformation: Critical Perspectives on a Theory in Progress*, Jack Mezirow (2000) defines transformational learning as the process by which we transform our taken-for-granted frames of reference (meaning perspectives, habits of mind, mind-sets) to make them more inclusive, discriminating, open, emotionally capable of change, and reflective so that they may generate beliefs and opinions that will prove more true or justified to guide action (pp. 7–8).

Although most of the conditions examined in the studies reviewed for this chapter focused on curricular conditions, within this body of research lie seeds which may inform student affairs practice for transformational learning. Faculty members may use critical dialogue focused on curricular content to situate students, their ideologies, and "their notions of fairness, in the larger, meta-narrative of human history" (Mayhew et al., 2010, p. 379); residence life staff may ask students to think about the ripple effects of their actions and those of others when developing community standards. Moving the dialogue held at floor meetings from one of justice as that which serves self to one that serves the broader community is one way to model advanced moral reasoning. Such modeling can be taken further in one-on-one interactions with students who may have violated community standards. Within a context of challenge and support, residence life staff may ask students to identify the reasons behind their actions and talk through the implications that result when reasons are grounded in serving oneself (preconventional) to one's friends and family (conventional) to the broader community (postconventional).

Clearly, one way student affairs practitioners can challenge and support students' journeys toward moral and ethical development is by asking students to integrate ideas and diverse perspectives across contexts (Mayhew et al., 2012a). Given the number of invitations to prominent (and controversial) public figures and thought leaders that have been rescinded in recent years, student union and activities staff may ask student programmers to consider the ethical dimensions as they pertain to the campus as a place of free speech and a marketplace for ideas (the political philosophy perspective), the power, privilege, and oppression context surrounding the controversial figure (the social justice perspective), the commitments to campus community and safety and how these commitments will be safeguarded before, during, and after the event (the legal, logistical, and pragmatic perspectives).

These are just two examples in which student affairs practitioners may use critical conversations in which students are asked to: (a) reflect on themselves and situate their ideologies within the broader context of justice in service of the public good, and (b) integrate diverse perspectives as a means to "articulate strategies for grappling with competing hypotheses and points of view" (Mayhew et al., 2012b, p. 42). Within a context of challenge and support, these and other approaches can be instrumental in creating transformative learning environments that foster students' journeys toward moral character development and wise and ethical stewardship.

References

Baxter Magolda, M. B., & King, P. M. (Eds.). (2004). *Learning partnerships: Theory and models of practice to education for self-authorship.* Sterling, VA: Stylus.

Bebeau, M., & Thoma, S. (2003). *Guide for DIT-2.* Minneapolis: University of Minnesota Press.

Bowman, N. A. (2009). College diversity courses and cognitive development among students from privileged and marginalized groups. *Journal of Diversity in Higher Education, 2,* 182–194.

Bowman, N. A. (2010a). Assessing learning and development among diverse college students. In S. Herzog (Ed.), *New Directions for Institutional Research: No. 145. Diversity and educational benefits: Expanding the scope, deepening our understanding* (pp. 53–71). San Francisco, CA: Jossey-Bass.

Bowman, N. A. (2010b). Can first-year college students accurately report their learning and development? *American Educational Research Journal, 47,* 466–496.

Kellogg Commission on the Future of State Land Grant Universities. (1997). *Returning to our roots: The student experience*. Washington, DC: National Association of State and Land Grant Colleges.

King, P. M. (2009). Principles of development and developmental change in theories of cognitive and moral development. *Journal of College Student Development, 50*(6), 597–620.

King, P. M., Kendall Brown, M., Lindsay, N. K., & VanHecke, J. R. (2007). Liberal arts student learning outcomes: An integrated approach. *About Campus, 12*(4), 2–9.

King, P. M., & Mayhew, M. J. (2002). Moral judgement development in higher education: Insights from the Defining Issues Test. *Journal of Moral Education, 31*(3), 247–270.

Lindsay, N. K., Barnhardt, C., DeGraw, J. E., King, P. M., & Baxter Magolda, M. B. (2007, April). *How college students interpret moral experiences: A mixed methods study*. Paper presented at the annual meeting of the American Educational Research Association, Chicago, IL.

Mayhew, M. J. (2012). A multilevel examination of the influence of institutional type on the moral reasoning development of first-year students. *Journal of Higher Education, 83*, 367–388.

Mayhew, M. J., Seifert, T. A., & Pascarella, E. T. (2010). A multi-institutional assessment of moral reasoning development among first-year students. *Review of Higher Education, 33*, 357–390.

Mayhew, M. J., Seifert, T. A., & Pascarella, E. T. (2012a). How the first year of college influences moral reasoning development for students in moral consolidation and moral transition. *Journal of College Student Development, 53*, 19–40.

Mayhew, M. J., Seifert, T. A., Pascarella, E. T., Nelson Laird, T. F., & Blaich, C. F. (2012b). Going deep into mechanisms for moral reasoning growth: How deep learning approaches affect moral reasoning development for first-year students. *Research in Higher Education, 53*(1), 26–46.

Mezirow, J. (Ed.). (2000). *Learning as transformation: Critical perspectives on a theory in progress*. San Francisco, CA: Jossey-Bass.

Padgett, R. D., Johnson, M. P., & Pascarella, E. T. (2012). First-generation undergraduate students and the impacts of the first year of college: Some additional evidence. *Journal of College Student Development, 53*, 243–266.

Pascarella, E. T., Seifert, T. A., & Blaich, C. (2010). How effective are the NSSE benchmarks in predicting important educational outcomes? *Change: The Magazine of Higher Education, 42*(1), 16–22.

Rest, J. R., Narvaez, D., Thoma, S. J., & Bebeau, M. (1999). DIT2: Devising and testing a revised instrument of moral judgment. *Journal of Educational Psychology, 91*(4), 644–659.

Salisbury, M. H. (2011, May). *Transformation or just a vacation: New evidence regarding the impact of study abroad on the educational outcomes of a liberal arts education*. Paper presented at the annual forum of the Association for Institutional Research, Toronto, ON.

Seifert, T. A., Goodman, K. M., Lindsay, N. K., Jorgensen, J. D., Wolniak, G. C., Pascarella, E. T., & Blaich, C. F. (2008). The effects of liberal arts experiences on liberal arts outcomes. *Research in Higher Education, 49*, 107–125.

Thomas, N. (2002). In search of wisdom: Liberal education for a changing world. *Liberal Education, 88*(4), 28–33.

TRICIA A. SEIFERT *is an assistant professor in the adult and higher education program at Montana State University.*

3

This chapter examines the findings, implications for practice, and directions for future research provided by the WNS research that focused on fraternities and sororities.

Research-Driven Practice in Fraternity and Sorority Life

Michael S. Hevel, Daniel A. Bureau

Few environments within American higher education evoke more polarizing perspectives than those related to fraternities and sororities. From their beginnings in the 19th century, college presidents and faculty members attempted to ban these organizations, arguing that they were incongruent within an educational community (e.g., Syrett, 2009). Even as the organizations took root on campuses across the country, these arguments endured (e.g., Maisel, 1990; Strange, 1986). Yet fraternities and sororities persisted because others within higher education passionately believed that they enhanced the educational experiences of their members. On any given campus, such supporters could include undergraduate fraternity/sorority members, student affairs professionals (especially those advising fraternal organizations), fundraising staff, and influential alumni, including board of trustee members.

Despite the divergent opinions related to educational value of fraternities and sororities, there has been limited research into how membership in these organizations influences students' developmental outcomes (Molasso, 2005). In part, this lack of evidence might be explained by the difficulty researchers face in determining whether educational outcomes resulted from membership in these organizations, from members' involvement in other activities on campus, or from who chose to join these organizations in the first place. In part, this lack of evidence might have resulted from the hesitancy of some fraternal stakeholders to learn how these organizations influenced their members' education, lest the results be unfavorable and support the claims of detractors. However, this attitude has begun to dissipate within the fraternal community. For example, when the second author started serving on the Association of Fraternity/Sorority Advisors (AFA) Executive Board, discussions about research and assessment were rare and tepid, particularly as umbrella groups—the councils governing the diverse collegiate fraternal organizations—were hesitant to

New Directions for Student Services, no. 147, Fall 2014 © 2014 Wiley Periodicals, Inc.
Published online in Wiley Online Library (wileyonlinelibrary.com) • DOI: 10.1002/ss.20098

participate. Today, many fraternal stakeholders, including umbrella organizations, are increasing their work with and embrace of evidence-based practice.

Fortunately, then, the Wabash National Study of Liberal Arts Education (WNS), a longitudinal research study that captured both students' development and their educational experiences three times—as they entered college, at the end of their first year of college, and at the end of their fourth year—has recently explored the effects of fraternal membership. In updating the literature related to the effects of fraternity/sorority membership, the WNS findings offer insights into the contemporary fraternal experience, provide implications for the practice of professionals working with these organizations, and reveal opportunities for future research. Indeed, professionals can use these results to implement a culture of research-driven practice in fraternity and sorority life.

WNS Contributions to the Scholarship on Fraternities and Sororities

The longitudinal design of the WNS makes it especially useful for studying fraternities and sororities. By capturing students' entering educational abilities, their high school activities, and their involvement at college, the WNS allows for a more precise isolation of the direct influences of fraternity and sorority membership than many earlier studies. This isolation is important because the individuals who join fraternities and sororities may differ significantly from students who do not affiliate. Without statistically accounting for these differences, educational outcomes may be mistakenly attributed to their fraternal experience.

The WNS has explored the effect of fraternity/sorority membership on a variety of outcomes—critical thinking, moral reasoning, intercultural competence, inclination to inquire and lifelong learning, psychological well-being, and leadership—associated with a liberal arts education. The results from the WNS provide an updated understanding of the influences of fraternity/sorority membership on educational outcomes in the early 21st century.

Research Results

This section synthesizes key research findings from the WNS on the impact of fraternity/sorority membership on college students' learning and development.

Critical Thinking.   Most of the research about the intellectual influences of fraternity and sorority membership has focused on GPA (e.g., DeBard & Sacks, 2011; Nelson, Halperin, Wasserman, Smith, & Graham, 2006) instead of cognitive development outcomes such as critical thinking. The National Survey of Student Learning provided a rare insight into

New Directions for Student Services • DOI: 10.1002/ss

the direct influences of fraternal membership on cognitive development, employing the critical thinking component of the Collegiate Assessment of Academic Proficiency and using longitudinal data from thousands of students attending 18 institutions. Fraternity membership was correlated with lower than expected critical thinking at the end of the first year of college, whereas sorority membership had no significant influence (Pascarella et al., 1996). By the end of the third year of college, the negative influence of fraternity membership had dissipated; neither fraternity nor sorority membership influenced students' critical thinking (Pascarella, Flowers, & Whitt, 2001).

Employing the same measure for critical thinking on a new generation of college students, the WNS found no direct effects of fraternity/sorority membership on critical thinking either at the end of the first year or at the end of the fourth year of college (Hevel, Martin, Weeden, & Pascarella, in press; Martin, Hevel, Asel, & Pascarella, 2011). While there were no direct effects, the WNS did reveal two conditional effects—an interaction between students' demographic characteristics and their fraternal membership influencing the educational outcome—related to critical thinking in the fourth year of college. White students who joined fraternities and sororities had lower than expected critical thinking (fraternal membership had no significant effect for Students of Color), and students who entered college with lower critical thinking skills (the bottom two thirds of the sample) and joined a fraternity or sorority also had significantly lower critical thinking scores.

Moral Reasoning.   Although several studies have shown that fraternity and sorority members are more likely than their unaffiliated peers to self-report academic dishonesty (e.g., Storch & Storch, 2002; Williams & Janosik, 2007), there have been relatively few investigations into the influence of fraternal membership on students' moral development. The handful of existing studies painted an inconsistent portrait. One study found that, at the time of joining, students who became members of fraternities had lower levels of moral reasoning than those who remained independent (Sanders, 1990); three studies found no significant effect on moral reasoning from joining a fraternal organization in the first year of college (Cohen, 1982; Marlow & Auvenshine, 1982; Sanders, 1990); and one longitudinal study found no statistical differences between those students who joined fraternities and sororities and those who remained independent, but, after two years of college, sorority membership was associated with lower levels of moral reasoning (Kilgannon & Erwin, 1992).

In updating these studies, the WNS revealed no direct effects on fraternity/sorority membership on students' moral reasoning in either the first or the fourth year of college (Hevel et al., in press; Martin et al., 2011). Like critical thinking, however, the WNS did reveal conditional effects related to moral reasoning and race in the fourth year of college. For White students, joining a fraternity or sorority was correlated with significantly higher levels of moral reasoning, whereas for Students of Color, fraternal membership was correlated with significantly lower levels of moral reasoning.

Intercultural Competence. As organizations that have historically segregated by race and remain segregated by sex, many educators do not perceive fraternities and sororities as environments that promote intercultural competence. Two earlier studies provided empirical evidence to support this perception, finding fraternity and sorority members with significantly lower intercultural competence than their unaffiliated peers (Antonio, 2001; Pascarella et al., 1996), but another study found that fraternity/sorority membership had no influence on intercultural competence (Rubin, Ainsworth, Cho, Turk, & Winn, 1999). More recently, a large study found that fraternity and sorority members demonstrated higher gains than unaffiliated students on the Enriching Educational Experiences Scale of the National Survey of Student Engagement (NSSE), which included interacting with diverse others (Bureau, Ryan, Ahren, Shoup, & Torres, 2011).

Employing two different scales that measured awareness, acceptance, and openness to diversity, the WNS found that fraternity and sorority membership had no significant influence on students' intercultural competence in college (Martin, Pascarella, Parker, & Blechschmidt, in press; Martin et al., 2011). These findings may challenge the prevailing assumption that fraternities and sororities inhibit the development of intercultural competence.

Inclination to Inquire and Lifelong Learning. The WNS was the first major investigation into the effects of fraternal membership on students' inclination to inquire and lifelong learning—an outcome that measures engagement in and enjoyment of challenging intellectual activities—although earlier studies explored related concepts. Some studies revealed that fraternity and sorority members demonstrated more academic effort or engagement than their unaffiliated peers (Pike, 2000; Pike & Askew, 1990). Other studies found fraternity and sorority members more focused on the extrinsic value of education (Astin, 1993; Wilder, McKeegan, Midkiff, Skelton, & Dunkerly, 1997), suggesting that such extra effort may be for future financial success rather than for the intrinsic value of learning.

In order to measure students' inclination to inquire and lifelong learning, the WNS used two scales: Need for Cognition Scale (assessing engagement in and enjoyment of difficult cognitive activities) and Positive Attitude Toward Literacy Scale (assessing enjoyment of literacy activities). Although the WNS found no direct effects of fraternity/sorority membership on these two measures at any point in college (Hevel et al., in press; Martin et al., 2011), students who entered college with the high levels of need for cognition (top one third of the sample) and joined a fraternity or sorority demonstrated higher than expected gains toward the end of college.

Psychological Well-Being. The WNS also offered the first insights into the effects of fraternal membership on students' psychological well-being. However, there were also earlier investigations relevant to this outcome and fraternal membership. Studies have found that students who participate in sorority recruitment have higher levels of self-esteem than women who do not participate and that fraternity men have higher self-esteem than unaffiliated men (Atlas & Morier, 1994; Brand & Dodd, 1998).

The WNS found neither direct nor conditional effects of fraternity/sorority membership on students' psychological well-being (Hevel et al., in press; Martin et al., 2011). Students were no better off—or worse off—psychologically from joining a fraternity or sorority in either the first year or fourth year of college.

Leadership.   The WNS has also explored the influence of fraternity/sorority membership on leadership skills. Indeed, of all the educational outcomes explored by the WNS, leadership is likely the one most commonly espoused by fraternal organizations. Perhaps not surprisingly, then, fraternity and sorority members performed well in most studies of leadership in the 20th century. Three studies revealed that students with prior leadership experiences or who placed more importance on leadership were more likely to join fraternities and sororities (Astin, 1977, 1993; Hughes & Winston, 1987). Once on campus, many studies found fraternity and sorority members demonstrated higher levels of involvement and engagement than their unaffiliated peers (e.g., Biddix, Matney, Norman, & Martin, 2014; Bureau et al., 2011; Hayek, Carini, O'Day, & Kuh, 2002). This elevated involvement appears to positively influence leadership skills, as other studies attributed fraternity and sorority membership to higher levels of leadership skills (e.g., Birkenbolz & Schumacher, 1994; Kezar & Moriarty, 2000; Kimbrough & Hutcheson, 1998). These studies mostly conceptualized leadership in "conventional" or "industrial" terms (Rogers, 2003), viewing leadership as a "top-down" approach, with individuals using power to control the people and organizations.

New conceptualizations of leadership became prominent in the 1990s. Instead of focusing on individual control, they emphasized relationships, shared goals, collaboration, and social responsibility (Rogers, 2003). The Social Change Model of Leadership (Higher Education Research Institute, 1996), operationalized by the Socially Responsible Leadership Scale (SRLS; Tyree, 1998), was designed under this new leadership paradigm and has become widely adopted by student affairs administrators and leadership educators. Would fraternities and sororities, with their presidents, executives boards, committees, not to mention their tendency to make decisions by majority vote, fare well under this new conceptualization of leadership? The earliest study related to the effects of fraternity/sorority membership on socially responsible leadership found that sorority women demonstrated significantly higher levels of leadership on seven of the SRLS subscales than fraternity men (Dugan, 2008). In a dissertation study, fraternity and sorority members demonstrated significantly higher levels of socially responsible leadership than uninvolved students and students who were minimally involved in other student organizations (Gerhardt, 2008). Given the design of these early investigations, it remained unclear if members' higher levels of socially responsible leadership were a result of different leadership skills at the time of joining these organizations or if fraternal membership contributed to higher leadership skills. The WNS was the first large study that allowed for the isolation of the direct effect of fraternity/sorority membership on socially responsible leadership.

The WNS found early gains in socially responsible leadership associated with fraternal membership that disappeared over the course of college. At the end of the first year, both fraternity and sorority membership was linked to positive growth on the citizenship subscale; fraternity membership was also associated with higher scores on the change subscale, whereas sorority membership was correlated with higher scores on the common purpose subscale (Martin, Hevel, & Pascarella, 2012). On the remaining five subscales, there were no significant differences attributable to fraternity/sorority membership. A follow-up study explored whether or not these early gains magnified, disappeared, or reversed by the fourth year of college (Hevel, Martin, & Pascarella, 2014). Unlike the first-year investigation, there were no significant differences on any of the eight SRLS subscales attributable to fraternity/sorority membership. An exploration into potential conditional effects—whether or not students who entered college with higher or lower levels of socially responsible leadership skills were differently influenced by fraternal membership—similarly resulted in no significant findings.

On the whole, the findings from the WNS suggest that fraternity and sorority membership today has little direct influence, positive or negative, on students' educational outcomes, at least among those outcomes studied here. Drawing implications for practice may be easiest when significant differences exist. However, a careful consideration of the WNS results related to fraternity/sorority membership reveals that there are practical implications from this statistical insignificance.

Using the WNS to Understand and Improve Fraternity and Sorority Life

Stakeholders in the fraternal movement—campus-based professionals, inter/national fraternity and sorority staff, alumni volunteers, and student members—can use the WNS results to better understand fraternities and sororities and inform their work with these organizations. Indeed, the findings of the WNS allow the exploration of three important questions: What does the WNS reveal about the fraternity/sorority experience in the early 21st century? How can these insights guide professional practice to improve the fraternity/sorority experience? And given this knowledge, what are the next questions for future researchers to consider? The answers to these questions illustrate how stakeholders can work together to help fraternity and sorority members realize important educational outcomes.

NEW DIRECTIONS FOR STUDENT SERVICES • DOI: 10.1002/ss

Understanding the Fraternal Experience.   Three key findings from the WNS provide important insights into the educational outcomes of the contemporary fraternal experience.

Fraternity/Sorority Membership Had Almost No Direct Effect on Students' Educational Outcomes.   On all educational outcomes explored by the WNS except leadership, fraternity/sorority membership had no direct effect. After controlling for students' entering educational abilities and for a host of potentially confounding experiences in college, the WNS found that joining a fraternity or sorority did not affect students' critical thinking, moral reasoning, inclination to inquire and lifelong learning, intercultural competence, and psychological well-being in either the first or fourth year of college. These findings run counter to the claims not only of fraternal critics who assert that fraternities and sororities are anti-intellectual environments, but also of fraternal proponents who argue that fraternities and sororities value scholarship and enhance the educational experiences of their members. The WNS suggests that fraternities and sororities may provide little influence, positive or negative, on the educational outcomes of their members.

Fraternity/Sorority Membership Contributed to Early, But Not Lasting, Gains in Students' Leadership Skills.   In the first year of college, fraternity and sorority membership was associated with significant gains in socially responsible leadership. However, by the fourth year of college, these significant differences attributable to fraternal membership had dissipated. This suggests that joining a fraternity or sorority provides students with early leadership gains, but that such gains do not persist throughout the college experience.

Students Can Experience Fraternity/Sorority Membership Differently. The presence of several conditional effects from the WNS revealed that fraternity/sorority membership can have different influences on specific groups of students. There were two types of conditional effects in the WNS, one based on students' entering academic abilities and one based on students' racial/ethnic identities. However, because most explorations of conditional effects revealed no significant differences, fraternity/sorority membership, on the whole, seldom influenced students' educational outcomes.

Improving the Fraternal Experience.   With these insights from the WNS in mind, what can be done to improve the fraternal experience? Considering this question raises implications for the practice for those working with the fraternity/sorority community.

Consider the Absence of Significant Findings.   The first step in extrapolating implications for practice from the WNS is to consider the lack of statistically significant effects of fraternity/sorority membership on students' educational outcomes. To a certain extent, no news is good news. Advocates of fraternities and sororities might find some comfort in that, unlike some earlier studies, there were no direct negative effects of fraternity/sorority membership. However, this does not allow advocates to promote these organizations as a value-added experience, at least in terms of these educational outcomes, as they have so often claimed. The investments in time and money that students put into the fraternal experiences, not to mention similar investments by institutions of higher education and inter/national fraternal organizations, suggest that stakeholders should be as intentional as possible in creating opportunities for undergraduate members to increase their development along key educational outcomes.

Connect Programming to Explicit Educational Outcomes.   Campus governing councils (e.g., Interfraternity Council), campus professionals, and inter/national staff members provide numerous programming opportunities for fraternity and sorority members. Many of these programs are planned with educational objectives and outcomes in mind. However, these learning outcomes may be more closely tied to understanding the responsibilities of a certain position or the specific policies of a campus or organization rather than overarching educational outcomes. Expanding these outcomes to incorporate broader developmental goals—improving critical thinking skills, fostering intellectual curiosity, enhancing broad leadership abilities—may improve the educational influence of belonging to fraternities and sororities.

Student development theory would be an especially helpful guide for educators augmenting existing and establishing new programs. By identifying a specific educational outcome that a program might foster, professionals can rely on a relevant theory to understand how individuals develop along the outcome and design appropriate educational activities. Risk management programs, often provided by both campus and inter/national staff, generally focus on educating members about specific policies and the importance of adhering to them. Programs that primarily provide rules from external authorities that are to be followed provide little incentive for their participants' moral development. Yet risk management policies are in place to protect individuals and the larger community, largely because of actions by earlier members that harmed the larger community (e.g., using chapter funds to purchase alcohol that played a role in a student death). This emphasis on community nicely aligns with theories of moral development (e.g., Gilligan, Kohlberg, Rest). Professionals should consider how to enhance risk management education to help members move from the preconventional level of "follow the rules" to higher levels of morality where they understand their responsibility to the larger organization and the need to ensure the dignity of all persons.

Focus Resources on the Least Academically Successful Members.   Fraternities and sororities, often at the chapter, campus, and national levels, celebrate and reward their most academically successful members. However, because the WNS found that fraternity and sorority members who entered college with dispositions to excel academically were advantaged by their fraternal membership while those with lower academic skills fared worse by joining fraternities and sororities, professionals should target the least academically inclined members for educational programs. The first step would be to identify at-risk students, perhaps by using their high school GPA and standardized test scores. Then professionals might identify "best practices" in scholarship programs and assess initiatives to identify what works on a specific campus or within a specific national organization. Given that academically inclined students were enhanced by their fraternal membership, incorporating these individuals into scholarship programs may be an efficient and effective way to improve the educational outcomes of all members.

Identify Educational Outcomes Most Relevant to the Fraternity/Sorority Experience. Although it would be hard to argue that the educational outcomes explored by the WNS are not worthy educational objectives, the WNS outcomes may not be the most relevant to the fraternity/sorority experience. Fraternities and sororities espouse "values development" as a primary outcome of membership, but to the extent that WNS outcomes measure these values, there is little evidence that today's fraternity/sorority experience has a significant influence on members' values development. Fraternal stakeholders might identify other outcomes more closely aligned with the purposes of fraternities and sororities. In order for these outcomes to have relevance in the increasingly evidence-based academy, fraternal stakeholders will need to identify measurable outcomes on which to assess the influence of membership through well-designed studies.

Use Institutional Resources to Gain Insights Into the Campus Fraternity/Sorority Community. While student affairs professionals at institutions that participated in the WNS received specific data about the educational influences of their fraternities and sororities, professionals at institutions where the WNS was not administered can still take advantage of local resources to better understand their fraternal community. Many more campuses employ the NSSE than participated in the WNS. Campus professionals can collaborate with institutional research offices to use the NSSE to examine how members of their fraternity/sorority community compare to nonmembers. In benchmarking the engagement of a campus's fraternity and sorority members with nonmembers, and possibly with the fraternity and sorority members at other institutions, campus professionals can learn the extent to which they need to partner with chapters and governing councils to improve members' educational involvement.

Directions for Future Research in Fraternity/Sorority Life. While the WNS findings provide some answers to guide research-driven practice in fraternity and sorority life, they also expose opportunities to better understand the influence of fraternal membership. Three key questions emerge from situating the WNS findings within the broader literature on these organizations. By exploring these questions, future researchers will provide even deeper understandings to help professionals address the challenges and realize the potential of fraternities and sororities.

How Can We Better Understand Diverse Experiences Within the Fraternity and Sorority Community? Today, the fraternity and sorority community is an increasingly diverse feature of American higher education.

Twenty-five years ago, most fraternity and sorority communities consisted only of traditionally White and historically Black organizations. Today there are "affinity" organizations focused on a variety of cultural heritages, such as Latino, Asian, and American Indian, and LGBT students and allies can join organizations such as Delta Lambda Phi. Organizations that bridge the professional and the social, such as Farmhouse and Triangle, are carving out niches to better support students' career goals. Groups historically found within academic departments, such as the coeducational business fraternity Delta Sigma Pi or the music-oriented Phi Mu Alpha Sinphonia, are becoming more similar to their "social" counterparts. The role of religion also remains important to some of these organizations. Historically Catholic, Jewish, Lutheran, and now Muslim students are connecting faith and fraternity. In addition to these diverse types of fraternal organizations, individual organizations are increasingly including more diverse members. While certainly not the case on every chapter on every campus, it is increasingly common for Students of Color and for openly LGBT students to join traditionally White organizations.

While fraternity/sorority communities are increasingly diverse, the WNS relied on a single item on the NSSE—"Are you a member of a social fraternity or sorority?"—to determine if participants belonged to a fraternity or sorority. The reliance on this item prevents investigations that center on the type of fraternity or sorority (e.g., traditionally White, historically Black, Latino/a) and the related conditional effects (e.g., the effect of fraternal membership on gay men who join traditionally White fraternities). Such studies are vital to further our understandings of the educational influences of fraternities and sororities, especially as campuses become increasingly diverse, host increasingly diverse types of fraternal organizations, and more diverse members join historically segregated organizations.

What Are the Environmental Conditions That Foster and Hinder Learning Outcomes Within Fraternities and Sororities?   Joining a fraternity or sorority provides students with many different opportunities—some optional and some mandatory, often varying among different organizational types and different inter/national organizations—and interactions with a variety of stakeholders. In short, belonging to a fraternity or sorority is a multilayered experience. These layers consist of environments that members go in and out of across the time of their membership, which include interactions with fellow chapter members and members of other fraternal organizations and experiences with campus administrators, chapter alumni, and inter/national organization staff (Barber, Espino, & Bureau, in press). If conditions must be right for students to learn in the college environment, what kind of fraternity/sorority experience is needed to foster learning? What kinds of experiences hinder student learning?

Future studies might examine individual layers of the fraternity/sorority experience to determine if they influence student learning and development. One area especially ripe for future research would be the influences of programmatic initiatives of inter/national organizations on students' educational outcomes (e.g., Biddix & Underwood, 2010). Many organizations have developed national programs focused on key concepts of the fraternity/sorority experience (e.g., Beta Theta Pi's "Men of Principle") that may have significant influences that become obscured when members become part of a larger survey sample of fraternity/sorority students who did not participate in such programming. Such studies might also help inter/national organizations enhance their programmatic initiatives.

Why Don't Fraternities and Sororities Influence Students' Educational Outcomes?   There is a perception among many educators and stakeholders that fraternity/sorority membership may be one of the most time-intensive experiences on a college campus, especially during the first years of membership. Because members often hold leadership positions within the chapter, pursue leadership opportunities outside of the chapter, live closely with one another in a chapter facility, and are expected to uphold organizational rules and standards, these organizations seem well positioned to influence students' educational outcomes. Advocates argue that these organizations provide life-changing experiences, foster meaningful relationships, and highly engage students. Therefore, the lack of evidence that fraternal membership influences students' educational outcomes should concern educators working with these organizations. How can membership and the related educational programs result in no significant difference?

Perhaps some activities commonly associated with fraternities and sororities, including binge drinking and hazing, offset any potential positive influence from these organizations. Future studies might work to isolate common features or activities of fraternities and sororities that might damper the educational potential of these organizations. Critics could claim that after all the investments made by campuses and inter/national organizations, no effect might be the "best" outcome possible from fraternal membership, while proponents of fraternities and sororities would like to see these organizations make a positive influence on the education of their members.

Of all the outcomes studied by the WNS, the one most likely to be influenced by fraternal membership might be leadership. The WNS results that found initial growth in leadership skills that disappeared by the fourth year of college may be explained by fraternities and sororities fostering involvement early in students' college careers, but that many fraternity and sorority members subsequently "check out" of their membership before their graduation. Although these members may continue to attend chapter meetings and social functions, they have long since passed on the leadership responsibilities to newer members. Subsequently, older members no longer build leadership abilities through their fraternal experience. Future studies could more closely trace when students begin to lose their leadership advantage by joining fraternities and sororities, giving practitioners ideas on how to best involve fraternal members at all stages of their college careers.

NEW DIRECTIONS FOR STUDENT SERVICES • DOI: 10.1002/ss

Toward Research-Driven Practice in Fraternity and Sorority Life

This chapter has explored how fraternity and sorority stakeholders can use research-driven practice to help their organizations become a more value-added experience on college campuses. To help students realize this goal, campus professionals and fraternity/sorority staff should develop the skills to provide guidance and counsel on areas such as academic programming, intercultural competence, and leadership development. As they advocate for these organizations, they must develop the skills needed to match the learning experiences of members with the espoused values of fraternities and sororities.

Students learn powerful, hopefully positive, lessons in college. In order to know the influences of fraternity/sorority membership on students' education, and in order to use that information to enhance their experiences, high-quality research must exist. The WNS findings can serve as a foundation for research-driven practice in fraternity and sorority life. Every higher education stakeholder shares a responsibility to facilitate student learning, and those who advise fraternity and sorority members have no greater obligation.

References

Antonio, A. (2001). Diversity and the influence of friendship groups in college. *Review of Higher Education, 25*, 63–89.

Astin, A. W. (1977). *Four critical years.* San Francisco, CA: Jossey-Bass.

Astin, A. W. (1993). *What matters in college? Four critical years revisited.* San Francisco, CA: Jossey-Bass.

Atlas, G., & Morier, D. (1994). The sorority rush process: Self-selection, acceptance criteria, and the effect of rejection. *Journal of College Student Development, 35*, 346–353.

Barber, J., Espino, M., & Bureau, D. (in press). Fraternities and sororities: Developing a compelling case for relevance in higher education. In P. A. Sasso & J. L. Devitis (Eds.), *Today's college students.* New York, NY: Peter Lang Press.

Biddix, J. P., Matney, M. M., Norman, E. M., & Martin, G. L. (2014). *The influence of fraternity and sorority involvement: A critical analysis of research (1996–2013)* [ASHE Higher Education Report, 39(6)]. San Francisco, CA: Jossey-Bass.

Biddix, J. P., & Underwood, R. (2010). A ten-year study of individual outcomes from a fraternity central office leadership program. *Oracle: The Research Journal of the Association of Fraternity/Sorority Advisors, 5*(2), 1–21.

Birkenbolz, R. J., & Schumacher, L. G. (1994). Leadership skills of college of agriculture graduates. *Journal of Agricultural Education, 35*(4), 1–8.

Brand, J. A., & Dodd, D. K. (1998). Self-esteem among college men as a function of Greek affiliation and year in college. *Journal of College Student Development, 39*, 611–615.

Bureau, D., Ryan, H. G., Ahren, C., Shoup, R., & Torres, V. (2011). Student learning in fraternities and sororities: Using NSSE data to describe members' participation in educationally meaningful activities in college. *Oracle: The Research Journal of the Association of Fraternity/Sorority Advisors, 6*(1), 1–22.

Cohen, E. R. (1982). Using the defining issues test to assess stage of moral development among sorority and fraternity members. *Journal of College Student Personnel, 23*, 324–328.

DeBard, R., & Sacks, C. (2011). Greek membership: The relationship with first-year academic performance. *Journal of College Student Retention, 13*, 109–126.

Dugan, J. P. (2008). Exploring relationships between fraternity and sorority membership and socially responsible leadership. *Oracle: The Research Journal of the Association of Fraternity Advisors, 3*(2), 16–25.

Gerhardt, C. (2008). *The social change model of leadership development: Differences in leadership development by levels of student involvement with various university student groups* (Unpublished doctoral dissertation). University of North Dakota, Grand Forks.

Hayek, J. C., Carini, R. M., O'Day, P. T., & Kuh, G. D. (2002). Triumph or tragedy: Comparing student engagement levels of members of Greek-letter organizations and other students. *Journal of College Student Development, 43*(5), 643–663.

Hevel, M. S., Martin, G. L., & Pascarella, E. T. (2014). Do fraternities and sororities still enhance socially responsible leadership? Evidence from the fourth year of college. *Journal of Student Affairs Research and Practice, 51*, 233–245.

Hevel, M. S., Martin, G. L., Weeden, D. D., & Pascarella, E. T. (in press). The effects of fraternity and sorority membership in the fourth year of college: A detrimental or value-added component of undergraduate education? *Journal of College Student Development.*

Higher Education Research Institute. (1996). *A social change model of leadership development: Guidebook version III.* College Park, MD: National Clearinghouse for Leadership Programs.

Hughes, M. J., & Winston, R. B., Jr. (1987). Effects of fraternity membership on interpersonal values. *Journal of College Student Development, 28*(5), 405–411.

Kezar, A., & Moriarty, D. (2000). Expanding our understanding of student leadership development: A study exploring gender and ethnic identity. *Journal of College Student Development, 41*, 55–69.

Kilgannon, S. M., & Erwin, T. D. (1992). A longitudinal study about the identity and moral development of Greek students. *Journal of College Student Development, 33*, 253–259.

Kimbrough, W. M., & Hutcheson, P. A. (1998). The impact of membership in Black Greek-letter organizations on Black students' involvement in collegiate activities and their development of leadership skills. *Journal of Negro Education, 67*(2), 96–105.

Maisel, J. M. (1990). Social fraternities and sororities are not conducive to the educational process. *NASPA Journal, 28*, 8–12.

Marlow, A. F., & Auvenshine, C. D. (1982). Greek membership: Its impact on the moral development of college freshmen. *Journal of College Student Personnel, 23*, 53–57.

Martin, G. L., Hevel, M. S., Asel, A. M., & Pascarella, E. T. (2011). New evidence of the effect of fraternity and sorority affiliation during the first year of college. *Journal of College Student Development, 52*, 543–559.

Martin, G. L., Hevel, M. S., & Pascarella, E. T. (2012). Do fraternities and sororities enhance socially responsible leadership? *Journal of Student Affairs Research and Practice, 49*, 267–284.

Martin, G. L., Pascarella, E. T., Parker, E., & Blechschmidt, S. (in press). Do fraternities and sororities inhibit intercultural competence? Findings from a four-year longitudinal study. *Journal of College Student Development.*

Molasso, W. R. (2005). A content analysis of a decade of fraternity/sorority scholarship in student affairs research journals. *Oracle: The Research Journal of the Association of Fraternity and Sorority Advisors, 1*, 1–9.

Nelson, S. M., Halperin, S., Wasserman, T. H., Smith, C., & Graham, P. (2006). Effects of fraternity/sorority membership and recruitment semester on GPA and retention.

Oracle: The Research Journal of the Association of Fraternity/Sorority Advisors, 2(1), 61–73.

Pascarella, E., Edison, M., Whitt, E. J., Nora, A., Hagedorn, L. S., & Terenzini, P. (1996). Cognitive effects of Greek affiliation during the first year of college. *NASPA Journal, 33*, 242–259.

Pascarella, E., Flowers, L., & Whitt, E. J. (2001). Cognitive effects of Greek affiliation in college: Additional evidence. *NASPA Journal, 38*(3), 280–301.

Pike, G. R. (2000). Membership in a fraternity or sorority, student engagement, and educational outcomes at AAU public research universities. *Journal of College Student Development, 44*, 369–382.

Pike, G., & Askew, J. (1990). The impact of fraternity or sorority membership on academic involvement and learning outcomes. *NASPA Journal, 28*, 13–19.

Rogers, J. L. (2003). Leadership. In S. R. Komives, D. B. Woodard, Jr., et al. (Eds.), *Student services: A handbook for the profession* (4th ed., pp. 447–465). San Francisco, CA: Jossey-Bass.

Rubin, D., Ainsworth, S., Cho, E., Turk, D., & Winn, L. (1999). Are Greek letter social organizations a factor in undergraduates' perceptions of international instructors? *International Journal of Intercultural Relations, 23*(1), 1–12.

Sanders, C. E. (1990). Moral reasoning of male freshmen. *Journal of College Student Development, 31*, 5–8.

Storch, E. A., & Storch, J. B. (2002). Fraternities, sororities, and academic dishonesty. *College Student Journal, 36*, 247–252.

Strange, C. C. (1986). Greek affiliation and goals of the academy: A commentary. *Journal of College Student Personnel, 27*, 519–523.

Syrett, N. L. (2009). *The company he keeps: A history of white college fraternities.* Chapel Hill: University of North Carolina Press.

Tyree, T. (1998). *Designing an instrument to measure socially responsible leadership using the social change model of leadership development* (Unpublished doctoral dissertation). University of Maryland-College Park, College Park.

Wilder, D. H., McKeegan, H. F., Midkiff, R. M., Jr., Skelton, R. C., & Dunkerly, R. E. (1997). The impact of Greek affiliation on students' educational objectives: Longitudinal change in Clark-Trow educational philosophies. *Research in Higher Education, 37*, 279–298.

Williams, A. E., & Janosik, S. M. (2007). An examination of academic dishonesty among sorority and nonsorority women. *Journal of College Student Development, 48*, 706–714.

MICHAEL S. HEVEL *is an assistant professor of higher education at the University of Arkansas.*

DANIEL A. BUREAU *is the director of student affairs learning and assessment at the University of Memphis.*

4

This chapter summarizes how diversity experiences influence college students' educational outcomes and offers recommendations for practice to maximize these benefits on all campuses.

Making Diversity Work to Improve College Student Learning

Kathleen M. Goodman, Nicholas A. Bowman

Diversity experiences, especially diversity in the curriculum and diverse interpersonal interactions, clearly have a positive effect on college student learning and development. Research has demonstrated this relationship repeatedly since the late 1990s (e.g., Gurin, 1999; Hurtado, 2007; Hurtado, Milem, Clayton-Pedersen, & Allen, 1999; Seifert, Goodman, King, & Baxter Magolda, 2010; Smith, 1997). Cognitive and psychosocial theories suggest that the mechanism that fosters learning and development is dissonance—an experience or new piece of knowledge that is inconsistent with how one typically thinks about things—which students often experience when they engage in diverse interactions or with diversity in the curriculum (Gurin, Dey, Hurtado, & Gurin, 2002). Despite the empirical and theoretical foundations supporting the premise that diversity can be catalyzed to improve learning, there is little evidence to suggest that colleges and universities have actually implemented the practices and policies necessary to make diversity work. While many colleges have implemented a diversity course requirement (Humphreys, 2000), there appears to be little coordinated and systematic effort to connect various diversity experiences and courses for improved student learning. A number of factors may hinder institutions from enacting diversity-related practices, not the least of which are the litigious and electoral efforts put forth by a substantial antidiversity movement led by organizations such as Center for Equal Opportunity, the Heritage Foundation, and the Center for Individual Rights (Cokorinos, 2003; Schmidt, 2006). The purpose of this chapter is to highlight findings from the Wabash National Study of Liberal Arts Education (WNS) that link diversity and student outcomes as well as to offer concrete suggestions for diversity-related practices and policies to improve learning and development for all students.

New Directions for Student Services, no. 147, Fall 2014 © 2014 Wiley Periodicals, Inc.
Published online in Wiley Online Library (wileyonlinelibrary.com) • DOI: 10.1002/ss.20099

Defining Diversity

Research has demonstrated that multiples types of diversity experiences likely affect learning and development. *Diversity interactions* are interpersonal encounters that occur across at least one form of difference, such as race, socioeconomic status, religion, or political orientation. To explore diversity interactions in WNS studies, researchers generally relied upon an index of 6–9 items reflecting how often the student engaged in diverse interactions. Examples of diverse interactions include: "had serious discussions with other students about different lifestyles and customs," "had serious discussions with other students about major social issues such as racial diversity, human rights, equality, or justice," or "made friends with students whose race is different from their own." *Attending a racial/cultural awareness workshop* was included in the diversity interactions index in some WNS studies and used as a separate predictor in others. *Diversity coursework* was generally defined as the total number of courses taken in the past year that focus on diverse cultures and perspectives (e.g., African-American studies, Latino studies), women's/gender studies, and equality/social justice.

Strengths of the Wabash Study

Many previous studies of diversity experiences used students' perceptions of their growth during college or asked students to report their skills or abilities at multiple time points in their college career. However, students' self-reported gains are highly inaccurate when compared with longitudinal assessments of student outcomes (e.g., Bowman, 2010a). The use of well-validated outcome measures is an important strength of the WNS that sets it apart from other large-scale studies. Furthermore, the use of a pretest–posttest design that takes into account students' entering levels on the various outcomes is an additional strength of the study, because it allows researchers to demonstrate change over time (Astin, 2003). As a result of these unique strengths, practitioners and researchers can feel confident in the findings reported in the following sections.

Diversity Works for All Students

In 1997, Daryl Smith set about to demonstrate that "diversity works" in a book with that title. She summarized research on the effects of campus diversity on students from 300 studies in higher education and found programs that emphasize interactions among diverse groups and opportunities to seriously engage with diversity issues in the curriculum contribute to educational success for both minority and majority students. In the 21st century, the WNS provided a substantial quantity of additional evidence that diversity continues to be positively associated with many college outcomes.

NEW DIRECTIONS FOR STUDENT SERVICES • DOI: 10.1002/ss

The WNS found that diversity interactions had positive effects on several cognitive outcomes, including need for cognition (a measure of one's interest in learning and complex thinking; Bowman, 2013; Goodman, 2011; Padgett et al., 2010; Seifert et al., 2010), positive attitude toward literacy (Loes, Salisbury, & Pascarella, 2013; Seifert et al., 2010), and critical thinking (Pascarella et al., 2014). Diversity interactions also predicted improvements in interpersonal outcomes such as socially responsible leadership (Bowman, 2013; Parker & Pascarella, 2012; Seifert et al., 2010), increased diversity interactions (Bowman, 2012), social/political activism (Pascarella, Salisbury, Martin, & Blaich, 2012), and intercultural effectiveness (Bowman, 2013; Salisbury & Goodman, 2009; Seifert et al., 2010). In fact, one study found that diversity interactions may lead to intercultural development even when those interactions are perceived as negative (Kendall Brown, 2008). Diversity coursework was also a positive predictor of many college outcomes within the WNS. Taking diversity-focused courses predicted increased need for cognition (Bowman, 2009), intercultural effectiveness (Bowman, 2010b), psychological well-being (Bowman, 2010b), and orientation toward social and political activism (Pascarella et al., 2014). In sum, these findings provide substantial evidence that "diversity works," in that diversity interactions and diversity coursework have been positively associated with many college outcomes.

Diversity Provides an Additional Boost for Some Students

While diversity appears to have a positive influence on learning and development for all students, the WNS has also provided considerable insight into how the relationships between diversity experiences and student outcomes vary based on student characteristics. For example, diversity interactions were associated with increased critical thinking skills among White students, but not Students of Color (Loes, Pascarella, & Umbach, 2012). In addition, diversity coursework and attending a racial/cultural awareness workshop were associated with greater need for cognition only among White students (Bowman, 2009; Goodman, 2011). White students have often had less precollege diversity exposure than have Students of Color, so these experiences were probably more novel and therefore more likely to contribute to cognitive growth. In addition, diversity interactions predicted critical thinking gains only among students with low or medium ACT scores (Loes et al., 2012; Pascarella et al., 2014). These authors suggested that diversity interactions may serve as a compensatory factor in fostering critical thinking skills among students who may have been less well-prepared academically upon entering college.

Differential effects also occurred based on socioeconomic status. Diversity coursework was more strongly related to need for cognition among lower income and first-generation students (Bowman, 2009; Goodman, 2011). However, Padgett et al. (2010) found no such difference for diversity

interactions and need for cognition, and Goodman (2011) also found that
the link between attending diversity workshops and need for cognition was
actually weaker among lower income and first-generation students. Finally,
Mayhew, Seifert, and Pascarella (2012) observed that diversity coursework
was positively related to moral reasoning only among students who entered
college in a transitional moral phase. These findings suggest that in some
cases, the gains from diversity are related to the developmental readiness of
the student.

Other WNS research explored conditional effects on noncognitive outcomes. Consistent with the results for cognitive outcomes, the link between
diversity coursework and students' well-being and intercultural effectiveness was stronger for White students than Students of Color (Bowman,
2010c), and the relationship between diversity interactions and political orientation was more pronounced for students with lower and medium ACT
scores than those with high scores (Pascarella et al., 2012). The relationship
between diversity coursework and intercultural development was stronger
among students from wealthier families (Bowman, 2010c), who may experience greater challenge—and subsequently greater growth—as a result
of their relatively privileged backgrounds. Diversity coursework predicted
increased social/political activism only among politically conservative and
moderate students, while diversity interactions were associated with increasingly liberal political views only among men (Pascarella et al., 2012).
Both of these patterns may have occurred because politically conservative
and male students were lower on those respective outcomes when entering
college and therefore had more opportunity for growth.

Regardless of these findings related to group characteristics, many studies that tested for conditional effects found none, suggesting that the potential impact of diversity is often similar across groups. For instance, there
were no conditional effects of diversity interactions, coursework, or workshops on literacy attitudes (Loes et al., 2013), and no systematic conditional
effects of diversity interactions on leadership and intercultural effectiveness
(Bowman, 2013). Moreover, the relationships among several types of diversity experiences were similar regardless of students' openness to diversity
and challenge (Bowman, 2012). Furthermore, WNS analyses have generally
tested whether the effects of diversity vary across *several* student characteristics (race, gender, precollege achievement, and the pretest) and yielded
few significant differences. In other words, these studies may have identified only one or two conditional effects among several possibilities. In short,
despite some notable exceptions, diversity experiences are often associated
with learning, development, and well-being for all students.

Sustained and Repeated Engagement Matters

Higher education research generally examines the linear relationship
between diversity experiences and outcomes, which is based on the

assumption that any increase in experiences will lead to improvement in student outcomes. However, there is reason to believe that infrequent exposure to diversity will have very little (if any) effect, because irregular and brief diversity experiences may not provide sufficient challenge to promote some types of student outcomes. Results of the WNS support this working theory.

Students who had zero diversity interactions actually had similar growth in leadership and psychological well-being as those who had rare or even moderately frequent diversity interactions (Bowman, 2013). In contrast, students who had very frequent interactions experienced considerable gains relative to those who had moderate diversity interactions. Similarly, taking only one diversity course was associated with no change—and sometimes even small decreases—in well-being and diversity orientations relative to taking no courses. However, students who took two or more diversity courses exhibited improved outcomes when compared with those who took no courses or only one course (Bowman, 2010b, 2010c).

Interestingly, although taking an initial diversity course may not lead to gains in psychosocial outcomes, it may contribute to cognitive growth. Students who had taken one diversity course had increased need for cognition relative to students with no courses, while taking additional courses was associated with very modest growth beyond the first course (Bowman, 2009). An initial diversity course may be sufficient to pique students' interest in relevant issues (and therefore their need for cognition), but it may not alter their deeply held values, skills, and well-being. Overall it appears that repeated or sustained college diversity experiences are often necessary to promote student learning and development.

Meaning Making and Nuances From a Qualitative Understanding of Diversity

While many qualitative studies examine a small number of students at a single institution, a strength of the WNS is that it includes interviews with hundreds of students at six colleges and universities. The qualitative data corroborate the quantitative findings related to diversity and provide some insights into how students make meaning of their diversity experiences.

When asked to identify significant or meaningful experiences during their first year of college, many students named interacting with diverse peers and being introduced to diverse perspectives as highly influential (Seifert et al., 2010). They said that encountering diverse ideas caused them to question their own assumptions and consider multiple perspectives (Jiang & Kendall Brown, 2008; Seifert et al., 2010). While this sometimes made them feel uncomfortable and/or uncertain about themselves, it also motivated them to want to learn more (Seifert et al., 2010).

When students engaged in diversity interactions that caused discomfort, they tended to follow one of three modes: they were unsure how to respond; they continued exploring the issues; or they reframed their perspectives toward a more advanced level of intercultural maturity (King, Baxter Magolda, & Masse, 2011). The mode they adapted was related to their developmental capacities; for instance, students' level of self-authorship was associated not only with how they make meaning of diversity interactions, but also the ways in which they engage in and respond to the interactions (DeGraw, Barber, & King, 2007; Kendall Brown, 2008; King & Baxter Magolda, 2007).

Diversity experiences were also related to institutional support. Although not all students reacted in the same way, some sought support through the organizational structures of their institution to help them make meaning of their experiences (Barber & King, 2007). Likewise, some students suggested that they needed to feel safe in order to explore intercultural differences and ultimately learn from them (King, Perez, & Shim, 2013). These findings suggest that institutions can play an integral role in supporting learning and development related to diversity.

Diversity-Related Practices and Policies to Improve Learning for All Students

As the research reviewed indicates, diversity interactions and diversity coursework predict many desired outcomes associated with attending college, including need for cognition, positive attitudes toward literacy, critical thinking, socially responsible leadership, increased diversity interactions, social/political activism, intercultural effectiveness, and psychological well-being. Diversity works as a catalyst for learning and development. Furthermore, while diversity may affect all students, it actually provides additional benefits for some groups that have had limited experience with diversity in their lives. Additionally, the more that engagement with diverse others and diverse ideas is repeated or sustained, the more students gain. Finally, the meaning-making process related to diversity experiences is mediated by and fosters increased complexity in developmental capacities. It is difficult to imagine any type of experience that has a broader and deeper impact on educational outcomes than diversity. Therefore, we suggest the following practices and policies to galvanize exposure to diversity through the curriculum and interacting with diverse others, in order to improve learning for all students.

Maintain a Strong Commitment to Diversity. As mentioned earlier, a highly organized, well-funded antidiversity movement is trying to prevent educators from focusing on diversity, which is described in detail in Cokorinos's (2003) *The Assault on Diversity*. This movement provides the infrastructure to challenge affirmative action through ballot initiatives, referenda, and litigation. As part of this movement, the Center for Individual Rights has sprung up to challenge the use of race for any purpose in colleges and universities, demanding that programs specifically designed for

Students of Color be dropped or made available to White students as well (Cokorinos, 2003; Schmidt, 2007). They are willing to use litigation as a means to enforce their demands. In the face of these efforts, institutions must remain committed to diversity because of the educational benefits it provides. Higher education leaders should use the considerable evidence about the educational benefits of diversity to maintain their diversity-related endeavors. Programs that support the success of Students of Color—a necessity at predominantly White institutions where Students of Color may feel marginalized—constitute a small part of an infrastructure that can lead to increased diversity interactions and increased learning for *all* students.

Diversify the Student Body. Logic dictates that it is not easy to interact with those who are different from you when the campus culture is monolithic. Evidence demonstrates that diverse interactions predict greater learning regardless of the type of diversity (e.g., Bowman, 2013). Therefore, we recommend recruiting and admitting students from different socioeconomic backgrounds, sexual orientations, political persuasions, and religious worldviews as an effective means to increase the heterogeneity of the campus. Additionally, increasing the racial diversity of the campus is also extremely valuable to the education enterprise. In the United States, neighborhoods and K–12 schools are quite racially segregated (Orfield, 2009), suggesting that many college students have not had the opportunity to engage across racial difference. Implementing policies and practices to increase all types of diversity on campus—including racial diversity—is a vital component to reaping the educational benefit of diversity.

Increase Opportunities for Engagement Across Differences. It is not sufficient to have a diverse student body if students do not engage with people who are different from themselves. Students need time in like-groups for all kinds of developmental reasons (Tatum, 2003). However, they must also be challenged to interact with those who are different from themselves. Institutions should provide structured opportunities for engaging across difference in many types of settings from the classroom to the residence hall and everywhere between. There are many resources to support intergroup and interfaith dialogue that can help guide dialogue (e.g., see www.ifyc.org and igr.umich.edu). Common practices on college campuses include panel discussions, lectures, debates, guest speakers, etc. While these are all wonderful ways to introduce students to diverse ideas, we suggest adding interactive sessions that provide opportunities for students to talk with individuals who may have different perspectives than their own. If you are bringing a nationally known political speaker such as Jimmy Carter, Karl Rove, or Colin Powell, start the session with an opportunity for students to talk with those seated near them about their own political beliefs and how they came to their political perspectives. If you are hosting a panel discussion on religious beliefs, take a break midway through in order to give students a chance to talk to one another about their own beliefs. Within the classroom, incorporating time for students to discuss their beliefs can be especially important, because engaging with other students whose opinions differ from one's own has been associated with increased need for cognition, whereas engaging with faculty and staff with differing opinions has not (Goodman, 2011).

Increase the Number of Diversity Courses.   Many colleges and universities have added a diversity course requirement to their general education plan. While this is a positive step toward increasing diversity awareness and knowledge, it can sometimes create problems as departments that typically provide diversity courses (such as ethnic studies, humanities, or social sciences) take on the burden of providing these courses for the whole campus. In addition, students who take only one diversity course may not receive some of the primary intended benefits of this coursework (Bowman, 2010c). Therefore, we suggest increasing the number of diversity courses offered, which will lessen the burden on any one department, increase the available course options, and promote student outcomes. For example, what if institutions provided an incentive for every major in the curriculum to include one course with a diversity focus as a requirement? Alternately, institutions could reward major and minor programs that include diversity perspectives in a certain percentage of their courses. For example, a department that incorporates diversity into 40% of their courses could be given additional funding for programming or travel.

Even on a smaller scale, it would be possible to introduce diverse perspectives in many non-diversity-related courses, if institutions provide appropriate encouragement, incentives, and guidance to departments. As a personal example, we often incorporate diversity examples into the research methods that we teach. Given the powerful effect that diversity courses have on learning and development, we suggest that colleges and universities give high priority to figuring out appropriate ways to increase diversity courses within the context of their campus culture.

Increase the Number of Diversity Workshops.   Increasing the number of diversity workshops focused on racial and cultural awareness has the ability to increase learning and development as well. Creating racial/cultural awareness workshops can use the expertise of your faculty or student affairs educators who are already conducting work related to racial diversity, interfaith initiatives, political perspectives, or LGBT populations. One approach would be to hold a regularly scheduled workshop at the same time each month so that it becomes ingrained as a regular event that students can count on. Another approach would be to develop a workshop and then work with others on campus to schedule times to facilitate it with extant groups (e.g., fraternity and sorority members, students in residence halls, honors students, student leaders, etc.). This approach would create the opportunity to centralize the workshop development process while using existing networks as a means of distribution. Regardless of how your institution pursues this goal, increasing the number of workshops may be a relatively easy undertaking (compared to curriculum revision) that could have a widespread impact on learning and development.

Provide Training and Support for Faculty and Staff.   To maximize the educational impact of diversity through the curriculum and cocurriculum, faculty and staff will need appropriate training and support. A survey could be used to pinpoint the expertise that is already available on campus. Qualified individuals could then be asked to provide trainings through existing faculty development structures. Faculty and staff could also lead small learning communities focused on "training the trainers" (helping others on campus learn how to incorporate diversity into their classes or develop workshops). The university library or multicultural affairs office could compile both an online and hardcopy collection that includes books, websites, online videos, and DVDs designed to help educators incorporate diversity in their work. There are also several national venues that provide training or opportunities for discussing the value of diversity, including:

- *Association for American Colleges and Universities (AAC&U)* (www.aacu.org) hosts a biannual conference on diversity and learning, publishes a quarterly *Diversity and Democracy* magazine for educators (which is free), and provides other programs and online resources related to diversity.
- *Interfaith Youth Core* (www.ifyc.org) provides resources about interfaith dialogue for faculty, staff, and students; hosts a campus religious and spiritual climate survey; provides sample syllabi; and provides consulting related to educational interfaith initiatives.
- *National Conference for Race and Ethnicity in American Higher Education (NCORE)* (www.ncore.ou.edu) provides a national forum focused on the complex task of creating and sustaining comprehensive institutional change designed to improve racial and ethnic relations on campus and to expand opportunities for educational access and success by culturally diverse, traditionally underrepresented populations.
- *Social Justice Training Institute* (www.sjti.org) provides diversity trainers and practitioners with an intensive laboratory experience where they can focus on their own learning and development to increase their multicultural competencies as social justice educators.

These are just a few of the resources that campuses can provide to faculty and staff to encourage and support the development of diversity within the curriculum and student interactions.

Ensure That Support Is Visible.   The effects of diversity on learning are powerful, but engaging in diversity can be challenging. Whatever steps your campus takes to increase diversity experiences, it is vital to provide visible support for students, faculty, and staff. Research has shown that some students will seek institutional support to help them make meaning of their diversity experiences; it is incumbent on institutions to provide the support for that meaning-making process in order for diversity to foster learning. Providing visible support also entails creating and maintaining safe spaces to engage in difficult dialogues.

Conclusion

Creating a campus environment that provides students the opportunity to have sustained and repeated engagement in diverse coursework and interactions has the potential to lead to gains in critical thinking, intercultural effectiveness, socially responsible leadership, need for cognition, psychological well-being, and other college outcomes. In order to galvanize diversity as a potent educational tool, we suggest that institutions recruit and admit students that increase the heterogeneity of the student body, increase the number of diversity courses and workshops on campus, and provide structured opportunities for students to engage across difference. We recognize that these endeavors require support for all involved. We suggest becoming acquainted with the research in order to justify and motivate diversity efforts; supporting faculty and administrators by providing access to the training and education they need to carry out these efforts; and creating a visible network of diversity advocates across campus so students, faculty, and administrators know where to seek support. Diversity can work as a powerful catalyst for learning for many students when institutions implement the policies and practices necessary to increase engagement with diversity.

References

Astin, A. W. (2003). Studying how college affects students: A personal history of the CIRP. *About Campus, 8*(3), 21–28.

Barber, J. P., & King, P. M. (2007, November). *Experiences that promote self-authorship: An analysis of the "demands" of developmentally effective experiences.* Paper presented at the annual conference of the Association of Higher Education, Louisville, KY.

Bowman, N. A. (2009). College diversity courses and cognitive development among students from privileged and marginalized groups. *Journal of Diversity in Higher Education, 2,* 182–194.

Bowman, N. A. (2010a). Can 1st-year college students accurately report their learning and development? *American Educational Research Journal, 47,* 466–496.

Bowman, N. A. (2010b). The development of psychological well-being among first-year college students. *Journal of College Student Development, 51,* 180–200.

Bowman, N. A. (2010c). Disequilibrium and resolution: The non-linear effects of diversity courses on well-being and orientations toward diversity. *Review of Higher Education, 33,* 543–568.

Bowman, N. A. (2012). Promoting sustained engagement with diversity: The reciprocal relationships between informal and formal college diversity experiences. *Review of Higher Education, 36,* 1–24.

Bowman, N. A. (2013). How much diversity is enough? The curvilinear relationship between college diversity interactions and first-year student outcomes. *Research in Higher Education, 54,* 874–894.

Cokorinos, L. (2003). *The assault on diversity: An organized challenge to racial and gender justice.* Lanham, MD: Rowman & Littlefield.

DeGraw, J. E., Barber, J. P., & King, P. M. (2007, April). *How diversity experiences contribute to deeper understanding of difference: A mixed methods study.* Paper presented at the annual meeting of the American Educational Research Association, Chicago, IL.

Goodman, K. M. (2011). *The influence of the campus climate for diversity on college students' need for cognition* (Unpublished doctoral dissertation). University of Iowa, Iowa City.

Gurin, P. (1999). Expert report of Patricia Gurin. In University of Michigan (Ed.), *The compelling need for diversity in education, Gratz et al., v Bollinger et al., No. 97-75237 and Grutter et al. v Bollinger et al., No. 97-75928.* Ann Arbor: University of Michigan. Retrieved from http://www.umich.edu/~urel/admissions/legal/expert/gurintoc.html

Gurin, P., Dey, E. L., Hurtado, S., & Gurin, G. (2002). Diversity and higher education: Theory and impact on educational outcomes. *Harvard Educational Review, 72*(3), 330–366.

Humphreys, D. (2000). National survey finds diversity requirements common around the country. *Diversity Digest.* Retrieved from http://www.diversityweb.org/digest/F00/survey.html

Hurtado, S. (2007). Linking diversity with the educational and civic missions of higher education. *Review of Higher Education, 30*(2), 185–196.

Hurtado, S., Milem, J. F., Clayton-Pedersen, A. R., & Allen, W. (1999). *Enacting diverse learning environments: Improving the climate for racial/ethnic diversity in higher education* [ASHE-ERIC Higher Education Reports, 26(8)]. Washington, DC: Graduate School of Education and Human Development, George Washington University.

Jiang, X., & Kendall Brown, M. (2008, November). *Learning through cross-cultural interactions: A developmental perspective on US and international students.* Paper presented at the annual conference of the Association for the Study of Higher Education, Jacksonville, FL.

Kendall Brown, M. (2008). *A mixed methods examination of college students' intercultural development* (Unpublished doctoral dissertation). University of Michigan, Ann Arbor.

King, P. M., & Baxter Magolda, M. B. (2007, November). *Experiences that promote self-authorship among students of color: Understanding and negotiating multiple perspectives.* Paper presented at the annual conference of the Association for the Study of Higher Education, Louisville, KY.

King, P. M., Baxter Magolda, M. B., & Masse, J. (2011). Maximizing learning from engaging across difference: The role of anxiety and meaning making. *Equity & Excellence in Education, 44,* 468–487.

King, P. M., Perez, R. J., & Shim, W. (2013). How college students experience intercultural learning: Key features and approaches. *Journal of Diversity in Higher Education, 6,* 69–83.

Loes, C., Pascarella, E., & Umbach, P. (2012). Effects of diversity experiences on critical thinking skills: Who benefits? *Journal of Higher Education, 83,* 1–25.

Loes, C. N., Salisbury, M. H., & Pascarella, E. T. (2013). Diversity experiences and attitudes toward literacy: Is there a link? *Journal of Higher Education, 84,* 834–865.

Mayhew, M. J., Seifert, T. A., & Pascarella, E. T. (2012). How the first year of college influences moral reasoning development for students in moral consolidation and moral transition. *Journal of College Student Development, 53,* 19–40.

Orfield, G. (2009). *Reviving the goal of an integrated society: A 21st century challenge.* Los Angeles: The Civil Rights Project/Proyecto Derechos Civiles at UCLA.

Padgett, R. D., Goodman, K. M., Johnson, M. P., Saichaie, K., Umbach, P. D., & Pascarella, E. T. (2010). The impact of college student socialization, social class, and race on need for cognition. In S. Herzog (Ed.), *New Directions for Institutional Research: No. 145. Diversity and educational benefits* (pp. 99–111). San Francisco, CA: Jossey-Bass.

Parker, E. T., & Pascarella, E. T. (2012, November). *Effects of diversity experiences on socially responsible leadership over four years of college.* Paper presented at the annual conference of the Association for the Study of Higher Education, Las Vegas, NV.

Pascarella, E. T., Martin, G. L., Hanson, J. M., Trolian, T. L., Gillig, B., & Blaich, C. (2014). Effects of diversity experiences on critical thinking skills over four years of college. *Journal of College Student Development, 55,* 86–92.

Pascarella, E. T., Salisbury, M. H., Martin, G. L., & Blaich, C. (2012). Some complexities in the effects of diversity experiences on orientation toward social/political activism and political views in the first year of college. *Journal of Higher Education, 83,* 467–496.

Salisbury, M., & Goodman, K. (2009). Educational practices that foster intercultural competence. *Diversity & Democracy, 12*(2), 12–13.

Schmidt, P. (2006, October 6). Minority journalists' program challenged. *The Chronicle of Higher Education, 53,* A22.

Schmidt, P. (2007). *Color and money: How rich White kids are winning the war over college affirmative action.* New York, NY: Palgrave Macmillan.

Seifert, T. A., Goodman, K. M., King, P. M., & Baxter Magolda, M. B. (2010). Using mixed methods to study first-year college impact on liberal arts learning outcomes. *Journal of Mixed Methods Research, 4*(3), 248–267.

Smith, D. G. (1997). *Diversity works: The emerging picture of how students benefit.* Washington, DC: Association of American Colleges and Universities.

Tatum, B. D. (2003). *Why are all the Black kids sitting together in the cafeteria? And other questions about race* (Rev. ed.). New York, NY: Basic Books.

KATHLEEN M. GOODMAN *is an assistant professor of student affairs in higher education at Miami University.*

NICHOLAS A. BOWMAN *is an assistant professor of higher education and student affairs at Bowling Green State University.*

NEW DIRECTIONS FOR STUDENT SERVICES • DOI: 10.1002/ss

5

This chapter explores how students' interactions with student affairs professionals influence college outcomes with a particular focus on applying findings to student affairs practice.

The Effects of Student Interactions With Student Affairs Professionals on College Outcomes

Georgianna L. Martin, Melandie McGee

In their seminal works cataloging three decades of research on the effects of college on students, Pascarella and Terenzini (1991, 2005) illustrate that experiences both inside and outside of the classroom influence how students learn, develop, and grow during the college years. Their synthesis of research overwhelmingly suggests that what happens outside of the classroom during college, traditionally the purview of student affairs programs and services, can have a beneficial or detrimental effect on students. Further, scholars have identified the tremendous influence that faculty and peers can have on students' growth during the college years (e.g., Astin, 1993).

Although scholars have identified how out-of-class experiences can affect students and how faculty or peers affect students, little research has explored the direct relationship between student affairs professionals and student learning and development. The purpose of this chapter is to present a new line of inquiry that seeks to address this gap in our understanding of the role of student affairs professionals in student development during the college years. Using findings from the Wabash National Study (WNS), this chapter will explore the direct impact of students' interactions with student affairs professionals on a variety of college outcomes including critical thinking, academic motivation, academic curiosity, attitude toward literacy, and social responsibility with a primary focus on applying these findings to student affairs practice.

Guiding Values in Student Affairs

Attending to the "whole student" has been a cornerstone of student affairs work since the beginning of the student personnel movement in the 1930s. The American Council on Education (ACE) convened in 1937 and

NEW DIRECTIONS FOR STUDENT SERVICES, no. 147, Fall 2014 © 2014 Wiley Periodicals, Inc.
Published online in Wiley Online Library (wileyonlinelibrary.com) • DOI: 10.1002/ss.20100

formulated, some would argue, the foundational document for personnel services, the *Student Personnel Point of View* (SPPV). The SPPV illustrated to educators that the whole college student was characterized by "his [sic] intellectual capacity and achievement, his emotional make-up, his physical condition, his social relationships, his vocational aptitudes and skills, his moral and religious values, his economic resources, and his aesthetic appreciation" (ACE, 1937, p. 1). Instead of primarily focusing only on intellectual growth, this viewpoint stressed the importance of developing students to become well-rounded individuals.

Several years later, the student affairs profession reassessed its role in promoting student growth. Documents sponsored or endorsed by student affairs professional organizations such as the *Student Learning Imperative* (SLI; American College Personnel Association [ACPA], 1996), *Powerful Partnerships* (American Association for Higher Education, ACPA, & National Association of Student Personnel Administrators [NASPA], 1998), *Learning Reconsidered* (Keeling, 2004), and *Learning Reconsidered 2* (Keeling, 2006) collectively were efforts intended to position student learning at the core of student affairs work. This emphasis on learning still articulates the fundamental vision of holistic student development etched out by the SPPV. Simply put, student affairs professionals are charged with developing students holistically, but student learning ought to be at the center of professionals' work.

Student learning, as defined here, is any variety of academic or cognitive gains such as grade performance, various forms of academic, intellectual, or cognitive development, and changes in learning-related attitudes or values (Terenzini, Pascarella, & Blimling, 1996). Cognitive competence can include such outcomes as critical thinking, intellectual flexibility, reflective judgment, complex meaning making, reasoning, comprehension, and independent judgment (Whitt & Miller, 1999).

College impact theories aim to address how and to what extent the college experience influences students' personal development and learning (Pascarella & Terenzini, 2005). For example, Pascarella and Terenzini presented a taxonomy of college learning outcomes in their synthesis of the research on the effects of college. The outcomes included in their text were verbal, quantitative, and subject area competence; cognitive growth; psychosocial growth; attitudes and values; moral development; persistence in college; career/employment outcomes; and quality of life following college. These are all outcomes that, at least anecdotally, most student affairs professionals would likely purport to cultivate in the college students with whom they work.

Measuring the Impact of Student Affairs Work

Although much of the research on how college affects students investigates how students' classroom experiences affect their learning, research on college students' out-of class experiences suggests that the classroom is not the only space in which students learn and grow. This comes as no surprise to student affairs professionals who regularly attest, at least anecdotally, to the learning that occurs outside of class.

"Out-of-class experiences" refer to structured and unstructured activities or conditions that are not directly part of an institution's formal, course-related, instructional processes (Terenzini et al., 1996). Overall, the literature examining students' out-of-class experiences reveals that several of these experiences result in positive outcomes. For example, living in a residence hall, an environment that is typically under the purview of student affairs professionals, appears to have a positive effect on students' academic achievement compared to students who lived in a fraternity/sorority house or in off-campus housing (Astin, 1993; Blimling, 1989). Further, out-of-class activities such as volunteering and leadership programming also have been associated with positive growth on cognitive-related outcomes in college (Astin, Sax, & Avalos, 1999; Kuh, 1995; Pascarella & Terenzini, 1991, 2005). Student participation in first-year experience programs and seminars has been identified as a "high-impact practice" for the benefits they offer students (Kuh, 2008).

These out-of-class experiences and others tend to be organized and supervised by student affairs professionals. Taking these findings together, we can assert that the work of student affairs professionals has an indirect effect on students' learning and development in college. In other words, many of the programs under the purview of student affairs professionals appear to have a positive impact on student learning, growth, and development. What the literature on the student experience seems to have neglected, however, is the direct impact that student affairs professionals may have on student learning.

The Missing Link? Exploring the Direct Effects of Student Affairs Professionals on Student Learning

Love (1995) drew attention to the omission of research on the direct effects of student affairs professionals nearly 20 years ago, noting the direct relationship to learning that scholars have identified with faculty and peers. Specifically, Astin's (1993) seminal work on the experiences that matter most in college identified students' interactions with faculty and peers as two powerful influences on student learning and development. Other researchers have reported positive associations between the nature and frequency of students' out-of-class contacts with faculty members and gains on measures of academic and cognitive development (Terenzini et al., 1996). Further, in their synthesis of the research on out-of-class experiences, Terenzini et al. (1996) found that students' interactions with their peers were consistently found to positively affect student outcomes. Peer teaching/tutoring, competitive peer environments, peer discussion of racial/ethnic issues, and socializing with various racial/ethnic groups are all activities that appear to have a positive influence on student learning and development. Love (1995) argued that researchers may be overlooking or excluding student affairs professionals from their frame of reference and this may explain why their influence has not been substantially assessed within the literature.

The absence of research on the impact of student affairs professionals and Love's (1995) call for increased research in this area, for the most part, remain unaddressed. Recognizing this absence in the literature, WNS researchers sought to begin addressing this void.

What We've Learned From the WNS

Using Astin's (1991) I–E–O (inputs, environment, outcomes) framework to guide their work, Martin and Seifert (2011) explored the direct effects of students' interactions with student affairs professionals on cognitive outcomes of college. In their study, they investigated first-year students participating in the 2006 and 2007 cohorts of the WNS. Martin and Seifert specifically focused on the impact of student affairs professionals on students' critical thinking, academic motivation, need for cognition, and attitude toward literacy during the first year of college. After controlling for a host of confounding variables (e.g., gender, race/ethnicity, parental education, high school ability, high school involvement, institutional type, and a pretest assessment for each measure) they found that as students increased their interactions with student affairs professionals, students decreased in their critical thinking score during the first year of college. Although the effect size for this finding was small in magnitude, the rigorous research design employed suggests that this remains an incriminating finding for student affairs professionals. On a positive note, however, Martin and Seifert found that increased interaction with student affairs professionals resulted in positive scores on measures of academic motivation, need for cognition or curiosity, and positive attitude toward literacy. Taken together, the three positive findings from this one study may highlight the role that student affairs professionals play in motivating students to realize their potential.

To add further nuance to this research, this study also considered the possibility that the effects of student affairs professionals might be mediated by particular experiences students have on campus. In particular, Martin and Seifert (2011) explored whether participation in an academic living-learning community, hours spent in cocurricular activities, holding a leadership position, and community service involvement mediated the effects of interactions with student affairs professionals. Interestingly, when Martin and Seifert considered these potential mediating variables, they found that the negative effect of student affairs professionals on critical thinking scores was reduced to nonsignificance. The researchers hypothesized that this change was likely due to participation in community service. In other words, at least for the students in the WNS, participation in community service mitigated any negative effects of interaction with professionals on critical thinking. Although this is hardly a ringing endorsement, this finding perhaps points to an out-of-class experience with potential to influence students' critical thinking in college.

Upon adding the mediating variables to the analysis, the positive significant findings on academic motivation, need for cognition, and attitude toward literacy remained significant. They did, however, decrease slightly in magnitude, suggesting that these positive findings are, in part, facilitated by activities such as living-learning communities, volunteering, holding a leadership position, and participating in cocurricular activities. That these positive findings persist in significance also may suggest that regardless of students' participation in select out-of-class activities, student affairs professionals have a unique and positive impact on outcomes like academic motivation, need for cognition (or intellectual curiosity), and attitude toward literacy during the first year of college.

Recognizing a need to further explore some of these concepts over the entirety of a students' college experience, Martin, Takewell, and Miller (2014) sought to replicate Martin and Seifert's (2011) study by investigating the impact of student affairs professionals in the fourth year of college. Similar to Martin and Seifert's research, Martin et al.'s study explored the impact of student affairs professionals on critical thinking, academic motivation, attitude toward literacy, and need for cognition. They found no significant effect on the impact of student affairs professionals on critical thinking over four years of college. However, they found that the significant positive relationship between interactions with student affairs professionals on academic motivation, positive attitude toward literacy, and need for cognition that Martin and Seifert found during the first year of college persisted in the fourth year of college. In other words, the study conducted in the fourth year of college replicates what prior research found during the first year of college, adding further credibility to the unique role of student affairs professionals in student learning and development. However, these findings over four years of college lead educators to speculate about other college outcomes that might be influenced, for better or worse, by students' interactions with student affairs professionals. Indeed, this is an area of research where there is much room for growth.

In addition to cognitive outcomes, researchers have explored whether students' leadership skills are affected by student affairs professionals. Martin (2013) used WNS data to investigate the direct effects of student affairs professionals on students' socially responsible leadership development in the first year of college. The measure used to assess socially responsible leadership, the Socially Responsible Leadership Scale revised version II (Tyree, 1998), is modeled after the Social Change Model of Leadership (SCM). The SCM is centered around individual, group, and community leadership values that help individuals actualize social change with an ultimate goal "to make a better world and a better society for self and others" (Higher Education Research Institute, 1996, p. 21).

Modeled after Martin and Seifert's (2011) study, Martin (2013) also controlled for a host of potentially confounding precollege variables. She also consolidated the "eight Cs" (consciousness of self, congruence, commitment, collaboration, common purpose, controversy with civility, citizenship, and change) of the SCM, measured in the SRLS, into the conceptual groupings described in the model: individual leadership, group leadership, community leadership, change, and an omnibus total score. Martin (2013) found that students' interactions with student affairs professionals had a significant and positive effect, if modest in magnitude, on all measures of leadership explored in this study. This study found what many student affairs professionals have likely believed for decades—student affairs professionals appear to enhance students' leadership development, at least as conceptualized by the SCM. It is also important to note that this study only explored these dynamics with students over the course of their first year in college. Time will tell if these significant and positive findings persist throughout a student's college career.

Implications for Student Affairs Practice

In the absence of empirical research on the direct effects of student affairs professionals on students' learning and development, professionals likely anecdotally assume that the one-to-one or group work they do advising, supervising, encouraging, and challenging students has a positive impact on college students. The line of research discussed here from the WNS mostly confirms what student affairs professionals believe to be true about the value and contribution of their work. In this section, we discuss ways in which professionals might use these findings in their work.

As evidenced by the research of Martin and Seifert (2011) and Martin et al. (2014), student affairs professionals appear to make a positive contribution to students' growth in curiosity, motivation, and attitude-based outcomes, including need for cognition, academic motivation, and positive attitude toward literacy. This may suggest a need for student affairs professionals to focus on ways in which they can strengthen the magnitude of this effect on college student development. In other words, if we know that these are outcomes where student affairs professionals already have a positive effect, perhaps a focus on how educators can strengthen the impact that they already seem to be having on students is an important step. These three outcomes in particular might be cultivated through mentoring opportunities. Departments and units within student affairs may consider developing structured opportunities for student affairs professionals to mentor students, particularly during key transition phases such as the transition to college, the transition to sophomore year, and the transition out of college. These transitory phases are times when students may need the support that student affairs professionals are poised to provide through motivation and encouragement.

Additionally, the positive findings across all measures of socially responsible leadership explored in Martin's (2013) study suggest a clear connection between students' interactions with student affairs professionals and students' growth in socially responsible leadership during the first year of college. In particular, students' group leadership values associated with socially responsible leadership (e.g., collaboration, common purpose, and controversy with civility) was the finding with the greatest magnitude, suggesting that professionals' largest contribution to students' development of socially responsible leadership might be in helping students learn to work effectively with others. This is a college outcome that receives relatively little attention in the larger body of literature on the impact of college. However, it is likely an outcome with a substantial connection to success postcollege since attributes such as being a collaborative "team player," ability to resolve conflict, and working toward an organizational goal tend to be sought after by employers in a variety of sectors. Student affairs professionals might also consider the ways in which they might strengthen their impact on students' growth in individual leadership and community leadership values. For example, facilitating opportunities for students to clarify their values and develop an ethic of personal integrity might further influence students' development along the individual values associated with socially responsible leadership.

In contrast, the negative finding that Martin and Seifert (2011) identified with critical thinking skills should cause educators to critically question not only the role that student affairs professionals play but also the developmental needs of students that might contribute to such a finding. For example, the first year of college is a time of transition for students—transition to collegiate academics, transition to living independent of parents or guardians, transition to living and working in close proximity with one's peers—that might require stability and support rather than challenge and growth in cognitively complex skills such as critical thinking. Perhaps it should not be surprising that students who receive the support and attention of student affairs professionals during this time of transition do not simultaneously grow in their critical thinking skills. This observation should not serve to recuse student affairs professionals from further exploring ways they might positively influence students' development of critical thinking skills. How professionals interact and engage with students may play an important role in students' college experiences and ultimately their success. Student affairs professionals at all levels ought to make critical reflective practice (Senge, 1990), or the act of reflecting on one's actions and behaviors through an improvement-oriented lens, a central part of their work.

We are unable to distinguish the types of student affairs professionals who students had in mind in responding to the survey items (i.e., we cannot differentiate between interactions with professionals in residence life versus student activities versus recreational services). While this reality limits the extent to which we can truly understand the implications of these findings for practice, it also leaves us wondering which student affairs professionals positively contribute to these particular academic outcomes. Knowing that students were referring to professionals in residence life or career services, for example, might give educators some indication of the types of functional areas with potential for improving students' growth in these areas. Conversely, knowing the types of functional areas that are not positively affecting students' learning and development might suggest areas for improvement in professional practice.

Conclusion

Implied in much of the discussion prompted in this chapter is the assumption that student affairs professionals *should* have a direct impact on college students' learning and development. In other words, is it enough for professionals to create, implement, improve, and maintain programs and services that benefit students without the individual professional being a direct benefit to student learning? The answer to this question may have implications for the future of student affairs as a field. Overall, these findings barely scratch the surface on the potential direct impact of student affairs professionals on students' learning, growth, and development. Academic motivation, socially responsible leadership, critical thinking, attitude toward literacy, and academic curiosity are just a few of the possible outcomes that student affairs professionals might influence. Without a doubt, this is an area that is primed for future research both in the breadth of outcomes explored and in the depth of understanding about the types of functional areas and interactions with student affairs professionals that inhibit or advance students' learning during the college years.

References

American Association for Higher Education, American College Personnel Association (ACPA), & National Association of Student Personnel Administrators (NASPA). (1998). *Powerful partnerships: A shared responsibility of learning.* Retrieved from http://www.acpa.nche.edu/powerful-partnerships-shared-responsibility-learning

American College Personnel Association (ACPA). (1996). *The student learning imperative: Implications for student affairs.* Washington, DC: Author. Retrieved from http://www.acpa.nche.edu/files/acpas-student-learning-imperativepdf

American Council on Education (ACE). (1937). *The student personnel point of view.* Retrieved from http://www.acpa.nche.edu/student-personnel-point-view-1937

Astin, A. W. (1991). *Assessment for excellence: The philosophy and practice of assessment and evaluation in higher education.* Phoenix, AZ: Oryx Press.

Astin, A. W. (1993). *What matters in college? Four critical years revisited.* San Francisco, CA: Jossey-Bass.

Astin, A. W., Sax, L. J., & Avalos, J. (1999). Long-term effects of volunteerism during the undergraduate years. *Review of Higher Education, 22*(2), 187–202.

Blimling, G. (1989). A meta-analysis of the influence of college residence halls on academic performance. *Journal of College Student Development, 30*, 298–308.

Higher Education Research Institute. (1996). *A social change model of leadership development: Guidebook version III.* College Park, MD: National Clearinghouse for Leadership Programs.

Keeling, R. P. (Ed.). (2004). *Learning reconsidered: A campus wide focus on the student experience.* Washington, DC: National Association of Student Personnel Administrators and American College Personnel Association.

Keeling, R. P. (Ed.). (2006). *Learning reconsidered 2: Implementing a campus wide focus on the student experience.* Washington, DC: American College Personnel Association and National Association of Student Personnel Administrators.

Kuh, G. D. (1995). The other curriculum: Out-of-class experiences associated with student learning and personal development. *Journal of Higher Education, 66*(2), 123–155.

Kuh, G. D. (2008). *High-impact educational practices: What they are, who has access to them, and why they matter.* Washington, DC: Association of American Colleges and Universities.

Love, P. (1995). Exploring the impact of student affairs professionals on student outcomes. *Journal of College Student Development, 36*, 162–170.

Martin, G. L. (2013). Measuring the impact of student interaction with student affairs professionals on socially responsible leadership development in the first year of college. *Journal of College & Character, 14*(4), 289–299.

Martin, G. L., & Seifert, T. (2011). The relationship between students' interactions with student affairs professionals and cognitive outcomes in the first year of college. *Journal of Student Affairs Research and Practice, 48*(4), 389–410.

Martin, G. L., Takewell, W. C., & Miller, A. (2014, April). *Value added? Exploring the educational effects of student affairs professionals.* Paper presented at the ACPA, College Student Educators International Annual Conference, Indianapolis, IN.

Pascarella, E. T., & Terenzini, P. (1991). *How college affects students: Findings and insights from twenty years of research.* San Francisco, CA: Jossey-Bass.

Pascarella, E. T., & Terenzini, P. (2005). *How college affects students, Vol. 2: A third decade of research.* San Francisco, CA: Jossey-Bass.

Senge, P. M. (1990). *The fifth discipline.* New York, NY: Doubleday.

Terenzini, P. T., Pascarella, E. T., & Blimling, G. (1996). Students' out-of-class experiences and their influence on learning and cognitive development: A literature review. *Journal of College and Student Development, 37*, 149–162.

Tyree, T. (1998). *Designing an instrument to measure socially responsible leadership using the social change model of leadership development* (Unpublished doctoral dissertation). University of Maryland-College Park, College Park.

Whitt, E., & Miller, T. (1999). Student learning outside the classroom: What does the research tell us? In E. Whitt (Ed.), *Student learning as student affairs work: Responding to our imperative* (pp. 51–62). Washington, DC: National Association of Student Personnel Administrators.

GEORGIANNA L. MARTIN *is an assistant professor of higher education and student affairs at the University of Southern Mississippi.*

MELANDIE MCGEE *is a doctoral student in higher education at the University of Southern Mississippi.*

NEW DIRECTIONS FOR STUDENT SERVICES • DOI: 10.1002/ss

6

This chapter uses findings on integration of learning from the qualitative portion of the WNS to discuss how students make connections between skills, ideas, and knowledge across contexts.

Exploring Students' Integration of Learning After Four Years of College

James P. Barber

Student affairs professionals are fortunate to have a perspective that allows for a close look at how students integrate learning. In our work advising student leaders, guiding campus organizations, and developing programs to enhance student learning, student affairs professionals often see (and sometimes help) college students connect learning from one context to another. I served in student affairs roles for many years and was privileged to frequently witness students' integration of learning: watching a fraternity treasurer use knowledge from his finance major to create a balanced budget, processing reentry with a student leader returning from study abroad who suddenly has new perspectives and priorities after traveling, seeing a resident assistant draw upon skills from a summer internship to do her job on campus better. This sort of learning fascinates me and drives my work as a faculty member, just as it did my practice in student affairs.

College graduates who are able to make connections among disparate information and meaningfully synthesize concepts are better prepared for success in the competitive and quickly evolving knowledge economy of the 21st century. In the past 25 years, increasing numbers of stakeholders have called for American college graduates to adeptly make connections among life experiences, academic curricula, and their accumulated knowledge (e.g., AAC&U, 2002; AAC&U & Carnegie Foundation, 2004; ACPA, 1994; Joint Task Force on Student Learning, 1998; Keeling, 2004). Of the seven liberal arts outcomes examined in the Wabash National Study (WNS), six were assessed by both validated quantitative instruments and in-depth student interviews. One outcome, integration of learning, was explored only using qualitative methods because there was not a validated instrument available. (For a discussion of all seven WNS liberal arts outcomes, see King, Kendall Brown, Lindsay, & VanHecke, 2007.)

NEW DIRECTIONS FOR STUDENT SERVICES, no. 147, Fall 2014 © 2014 Wiley Periodicals, Inc.
Published online in Wiley Online Library (wileyonlinelibrary.com) • DOI: 10.1002/ss.20101

I have developed the following definition of integration of learning, drawing from the various definitions discovered in a review of empirical research and my own analyses of the WNS qualitative data:

> Integration of learning is the demonstrated ability to connect, apply, and/or synthesize information coherently from disparate contexts and perspectives, and make use of these new insights in multiple contexts. This includes the ability to connect the domain of ideas and philosophies to the everyday experience, from one field of study or discipline to another, from the past to the present, between campus and community life, from one part to the whole, from the abstract to the concrete, among multiple identity roles—and vice versa. (Barber, 2012, p. 593)

Despite enthusiasm about integration of learning from both educators and employers, there is a lack of detailed information about the ways in which college students develop this outcome. This chapter explores how integration of learning develops for three traditional-aged college students from their freshman to senior years and discusses how student affairs professionals can use the methods and findings to improve their work through research-driven practice.

Theoretical Framework

The self-authorship developmental model and the integration of learning construct serve as components of my theoretical framework. Self-authorship is a holistic model describing how individuals grow and change in the ways they make meaning of knowledge, identity, and relationships with others (Baxter Magolda, 1998, 2001; Kegan, 1994). Research demonstrates that there is a developmental trajectory toward self-authorship from a reliance on externally driven ways of thinking to more internally derived meaning making (Baxter Magolda, 1999, 2001; Kegan, 1994). This model offers a perspective that informs inquiry into the development of integration of learning. Previous analyses indicate there is a similar developmental process in relation to integration of learning (Barber, 2014).

Integration of learning describes the process by which individuals bring together experience, knowledge, and skills across contexts. Three major categories of integration of learning have emerged from empirical research, listed here in order of increasing complexity: (a) *Connection*, the discovery of a similarity between ideas which themselves remain distinctive; (b) *Application*, the use of knowledge from one context in another; and (c) *Synthesis*, the creation of new knowledge by combining two or more insights (Barber, 2012). As students advance developmentally along the self-authorship continuum, they integrate learning more frequently and use these three categories of integration in concert (Barber, 2009, 2014).

NEW DIRECTIONS FOR STUDENT SERVICES • DOI: 10.1002/ss

Methods

As summarized in Chapter 1 of this volume, the WNS used a longitudinal concurrent mixed methods design in which two independent strands of data (surveys and interviews) were collected for addressing related but separate research questions. The illustrative analytic sample that I use for this chapter is comprised of three participants who completed interviews each of their four undergraduate years ($n = 12$ interviews). The longitudinal structure of the WNS allows a rare opportunity to examine an individual's development over time in detail. Each *longitudinal interview set* documents a unique student's college experience over four years; each interview set is composed of four interviews totaling approximately six hours or 100 transcribed pages per student. Previous research investigating self-authorship has shown the in-depth case study approach to be useful for examining the nuances of learning and development over a period of several years (Barber & King, 2014; Barber, King, & Baxter Magolda, 2013; Baxter Magolda, 2009; Baxter Magolda & King, 2012). Lincoln and Guba's (1985) substantive case report format provides a template for considering the findings of the current analysis of four-year student interview sets.

To illustrate integration of learning for this chapter, I selected interviews from those collected at two of the six interview campuses in the longitudinal study, Hudson College (pseudonym) and Wabash College (actual name). I chose these two campuses based on the richness of the student interview data, and because these sites offered a variety of experiences in both curricular and cocurricular settings that were intentionally designed to promote integration of learning. I visited each campus personally and collected interviews on site, which provided me a deeper understanding of their campus contexts. I chose the three individuals for this chapter using a number of criteria. I sought students who: (a) participated in WNS interviews all four years; (b) had rich conversations that offered clear examples of integration of learning; (c) discussed the same or similar experiences each year, so as to provide a common thread through the four interviews for purposes of comparison; and (d) represented diversity in terms of gender, race, ethnicity, and institution.

Campus Contexts.   Hudson College is a private, coeducational institution that enrolls approximately 1,600 undergraduates. It offers two academic programs that are of interest to this study of integration of learning: the *Liberal Arts Workshop* and the *Freshman Symposium*. The *Liberal Arts Workshop* is an intentionally integrative program in which students participate for the three weeks immediately preceding their first year in college. The aims of this program are for students to learn to read and listen more thoughtfully, to express ideas, to review their own work critically, and to recognize the link between thinking and expressing. The curriculum of this program culminates in a written assignment that a student must pass in order to matriculate. Upon matriculating to the college, all students must

New Directions for Student Services • DOI: 10.1002/ss

enroll in *Freshman Symposium*, a two-semester sequence focused on important cultural and intellectual ideas that the institution believes form a basis for liberal arts education.

Wabash College is an all-male private liberal arts college in rural Indiana enrolling approximately 900 students. The *Freshman Tutorial* is a program at Wabash that is of interest in terms of integration of learning; all students take this course during their first year. Each section enrolls approximately 15 students. The main objective of the *Freshman Tutorial* is to give students the skills they need to be critical thinkers, successful in a discussion-based seminar environment, and well-prepared for the intensity of college writing. This course is followed in the second year with a two-semester sequence on classic world texts called *Cultures and Traditions*, a requirement for all sophomores.

Data Analysis.   Each interview was independently analyzed for self-authorship and integration of learning. Working from the complete interview transcripts, trained research team members assessed self-authorship level for each of the four years of the study, beginning by identifying important developmental experiences discussed in each interview. The determination of developmental impact is particularly important for understanding developmental changes. Team members determined whether an experience was "developmentally effective," meaning whether it had a positive impact on students' development toward self-authorship (King, Baxter Magolda, Barber, Kendall Brown, & Lindsay, 2009, p. 109). By analyzing these experiences, researchers were able to identify characteristics of experiences that transformed students' approaches to meaning making and better understand developmental mechanisms (King et al., 2009).

Self-authorship assessment was guided by the WNS theoretical framework and contemporary research, resulting in the creation of a 10-position continuum (Baxter Magolda & King, 2012). This continuum reflects the gradual movement of external forces to the background and the internal voice to the foreground. The continuum uses "E" to represent external and "I" to symbolize internal, including three positions within solely external voice [Ea, Eb, Ec], two positions within predominantly external voice (also called entering the crossroads) [E(I), E–I,], two positions within predominantly internal voice (or leaving the crossroads) [I–E, I(E)], and three positions within solely internal voice (i.e., self-authorship) [Ia, Ib, Ic] (see Table 6.1 for additional detail).

Examples of integration of learning were identified, and subsequently scrutinized and categorized using the constant comparative method advocated in grounded theory (Charmaz, 2006; Glaser & Strauss, 1967). I used grounded theory to analyze the data in order to allow *the ways* students integrate learning and *how they make meaning* of that process to emerge from the data rather than to establish a priori the characteristics and categories of this developmental process (Glaser & Strauss, 1967; Strauss & Corbin, 1998). Analyses of the interview data suggest an increasing complexity in

Table 6.1. Developmental Positions in the Journey Toward Self-Authorship

Developmental Position	Key Characteristics
Ea: Solely external	Consistently and unquestioningly rely on external sources *without recognizing* possible shortcomings of this approach.
Eb: Solely external	Consistently rely on external sources but *experience tensions* in doing so, particularly if external sources conflict; look to authorities to resolve these conflicts.
Ec: Solely external	Continue to rely on external sources but *recognize shortcomings* of this approach.
E(I): Entering the crossroads	Continue to rely on external sources despite *awareness of the need* for an internal voice. Realize the dilemma of external meaning making, yet are unsure how to proceed.
E–I: Entering the crossroads	Begin to *actively work on constructing* a new way of making meaning, yet "lean back" to earlier external positions.
I–E: Leaving the crossroads	Begin to *listen carefully* to internal voice, which now edges out external sources. External sources still strong, making it hard to maintain the internal voice consistently.
I(E): Leaving the crossroads	Actively work to *cultivate* the internal voice, which mediates most external sources. Consciously work to not slip back into former tendency to allow others' points of view to subsume own point of view.
Ia: Solely internal	*Trust* the internal voice sufficiently to refine beliefs, values, identities, and relationships. Use internal voice to shape reactions and manage external sources.
Ib: Solely internal	Trust internal voice sufficiently to craft commitments into a *philosophy of life* to guide how to react to external sources.
Ic: Solely internal	Solidify philosophy of life as the *core of one's being*; living it becomes second nature.

Note. Adapted from "Assessing Meaning Making and Self-Authorship: Theory, Research, and Application," by M. B. Baxter Magolda and P. M. King, 2012, *ASHE Higher Education Report Series*, 38(3), p. 19. Copyright 2012 by Jossey-Bass. Reprinted with permission.

students' integration of learning over time (Barber, 2012, 2014), similar to the developmental pattern established in self-authorship research (Baxter Magolda, 1998, 2001; Baxter Magolda & King, 2012).

Finally, the assessments of both self-authorship and integration of learning were contextualized to each individual and his or her campus. Reviewing a particular student's data holistically as an interview set that spanned his or her freshman, sophomore, junior, and senior years allowed me to uncover trends in student learning and development not apparent in separate annual interviews.

Limitations.   This study includes students on two campuses that are small, private, liberal arts colleges in rural settings. Both had intentionally integrative programs for first-year students established at their institutions (*Liberal Arts Workshop* and *Freshman Symposium* at Hudson; *Freshman Tutorial* courses and *Cultures and Traditions* sequence at Wabash), and both were selected for the larger WNS based on interest in and programs on liberal arts education.

The similar ages of students in the sample (all were traditionally aged college students, 18–22 years old) may also have limited the types of integration I observed in the interviews. It is to be expected that students early in college will have less complex ways of thinking than more advanced students (Baxter Magolda, 1999; Kegan, 1994).

Findings

I illustrate the findings using excerpts from longitudinal interviews with three students:[1] Reese, a White woman attending Hudson College; Kayla, an international student at Hudson; and Steve, a White student enrolled at Wabash College. Each student participated in the WNS interview all four years in college.

Reese: Building on Camp Counselor Experiences.   In Reese's first-year interview, she described her entry to college, and how she was connecting her previous experiences to her new life as a college student. In this conversation, Reese introduced the interviewer to her experiences with summer camp, initially as a participant and later as a counselor.

> [College] kind of seems like . . . a bigger version of high school. . . . It just seems like I'm taking my home life, I'm taking my interests, and taking them with me . . . so it's kind of like taking what I've loved from my whole life and bringing that to college, but seeing what else is out there.

Reese's self-authorship orientation during her first year was assessed as Eb on the developmental continuum. She was able to integrate learning superficially, connecting her college life to her high school experiences by describing activities mirrored in both.

In her second-year interview, Reese returned to her experience at camp, this time discussing how she was applying the Hebrew language skills learned at the camp to her study of Hebrew in college. The ways in which she integrated her learning were more complex this year, as was her self-authorship orientation, which had advanced to E(I).

> But I know how to read it [Hebrew]. And camp actually has taught me a lot, going into it. I know so many vocabulary words from camp. And some

phrases that the Israelis have taught me. You know piecing things together. So it's helped in the beginning of the class. And now it's starting to actually pick up to the things that I might not know. So it's good.

By her junior year, Reese described how she was applying what she had learned in camp (her "skills" with kids) to a new position teaching at a local Jewish Foundation. Note the larger scope of Reese's integration as she began to think about how her work with children at camp influenced her thoughts about a future career path. Her developmental level has shifted to I–E as she begins to listen to the internal voice.

I'm teaching youth school at the [Congregation] Jewish Foundation. They're four fourth graders, but it's fun to be in charge of that and to work with them and I've gotten involved. . . . It was a 45-minute program and I just wanted to kind of hang out, so that was kind of like putting my skills [from camp] into action, but it was hard. . . .I think I will [go into teaching]. I like kids. I think teaching is a lot of fun and, and I definitely, I mean I would want to teach elementary school kids because I would get to teach different subjects and I don't know if I want to tie myself down to one subject.

Finally, in her senior-year interview, Reese talked about how she used the interpersonal skills she gained as a camp counselor to build relationships with other students during a five-month study abroad trip to Israel during her junior year. She was able to build a peer support system quickly and was at ease negotiating relationships. During her time abroad, she also applied the Hebrew language skills gained from her work at camp and classroom language studies.

I make friends pretty easily, having gone to camp and things like that, when you're put in a situation when you're only going to be there for a certain amount of time, I think anybody does this, you negotiate this space differently. You negotiate making friends and develop trust in friendships a little bit more quickly than you normally would. So I think, just from that aspect I made friends pretty quickly and you start trusting people. Well, at least I do. You know, more quickly because if you need that support system, you need somebody that you're going to trust or talk to about things. I think it just develops the relationship quicker, too, talking about certain things, back and forth and developing that trust more quickly allows you to have that support system.

Reese demonstrated development in terms of self-authorship in college, with an assessment in her senior year of I(E), indicating active work in cultivating her internal voice. The frequency of her integration of learning increased over time as well, moving from five examples of integration in her freshman year to nine examples during her final interview. (The

Table 6.2.   Student Data on Frequency of Integration of Learning and Developmental Position, by Year

Student	Frequency of IOL (Examples per Interview)				Developmental Position			
	Y1	Y2	Y3	Y4	Y1	Y2	Y3	Y4
Reese	5	4	5	9	Eb	E(I)	I–E	I(E)
Kayla	2	6	3	9	Ea	Eb	I–E	E–I
Steve	2	5	5	9	Eb	E(I)	I(E)	Ia

frequency of integration of learning and the self-authorship assessment for each student, in each of the four years, are presented in Table 6.2.)

Kayla: International Student, Researcher, and Citizen.   Kayla is an international student who attended Hudson College. She is of Korean descent, although her family has lived in India for a number of years. Kayla discussed her thoughts about coursework often during her four interviews, and this common thread provided a window into her ability to integrate learning. As a first-year student, her self-authorship assessment was Ea on the developmental continuum, indicating a reliance on authorities. In her first-year interview, she described her experience with Hudson's *Liberal Arts Workshop* (also known as LAW), an intensive three-week academic session for new students in the summer, immediately before matriculation.

> There were lots of parts, a lot of free writing, which is a concept I knew of before because I did that in high school. . . . But the entire LAW program sort of opened me up towards writing. . . . I just kept writing, writing, writing! So, if you just tell me to write something now, I'll just start writing. So that, and my LAW teacher made sure that she instilled some confidence in me about my writing. I also was not a very creative person back in high school. . . . I think I'm not able to think outside of the box, because I'm just so used to like the first nine years of my education, just being used to having everything spoon fed, and, and having been told that this is what is right. And so, I'm trying to think out of the box more, but I just find myself sort of connecting two far apart, like, drawn out things together.

Kayla attended a boarding high school in India, and connected her learning experiences there (particularly, writing) to her initial experiences in the *Liberal Arts Workshop* at Hudson.

At the beginning of her sophomore year, Kayla's developmental level had increased slightly to Eb. In her second interview, Kayla revisited her academics and writing in response to a question asking about her most important experience in the past year. She replied,

Most important time in terms of academics I think is the B+ I got on my final *Freshman Symposium* paper for first semester. Because it's the first time I got a B+ after this series of C's and D's I got for my *Freshman Symposium*. And I think it was, even if it wasn't an A, I worked very hard for that B+ and I knew, I could just by seeing, comparing my writing from LAW to my *Freshman Symposium* paper I could see, wow, I improved...that has helped me come over my fear of writing to some extent, that B+, so that was very significant in terms of my academic career.

Kayla was applying the skills she learned as a new student in the *Liberal Arts Workshop* to her later work in college. The confidence she gained as a first-year student grew, and she was able to recognize her progress and integrate what she learned in a new context as a sophomore.

By her third year, Kayla described integration of learning beyond application of writing skills. Her developmental assessment shifted to I–E on the self-authorship continuum as she began to listen to her internal voice. Kayla was very excited about her recent acceptance to participate in a Hudson College study abroad research trip to Tibet, a region of China. She described how she was preparing for this excursion:

It's going to be interviewing other people and just asking them questions and sort of collecting data and things like that. So I think it's going to be really new, maybe things I've learned in my *Economics of Developing Nations* class would help. Maybe my basic micro macro [economics] which I've forgotten most of it maybe [laughs] it might help. . . . The other three students are all Hudsonian [from Kayla's same institution] and my Chinese professor told me about this research and she knew that I was very active in *Students for a Free Tibet* [an international student organization with a chapter at Hudson] things and so she said, "Oh I think you would bring a very interesting perspective to the group, seeing your activities back at school." Of course I can. . . . I'm very excited.

Whereas at the beginning of her sophomore year Kayla talked primarily about building her confidence in writing and applying her newly acquired writing skills across course contexts, as she prepared for her junior year, the integration was much broader. Her study abroad research trip created an opportunity for her to draw on previous economics courses and out-of-class experiences as a member of *Students for a Free Tibet* to develop her research questions.

In her final interview, Kayla talked about the experiences she had in China, and continued to integrate knowledge and skills broadly across contexts. Her developmental assessment decreased slightly from the previous year to E–I, still placing her in the crossroads phase of the journey toward self-authorship and indicating ongoing, active work on constructing a new

NEW DIRECTIONS FOR STUDENT SERVICES • DOI: 10.1002/ss

way of making meaning. She credited Hudson College with providing experiences that facilitated her learning and provided the following examples:

> [Hudson College] has definitely influenced the way I look at things. And I guess more confident of my judgments and my opinions . . . because we have great class discussions. And I felt like there was a lot to learn from my fellow students and that kind of an environment. So it definitely influenced the way I look at things. And there's things I also learn at class. Some of my professors and also from my readings changed the way I look at things. . . . I had a professor from Zimbabwe for my international relations class and . . . it definitely helped me understand the overarching situation in Africa much better. . . . . From my various outside of Hudson experiences to my internships and research trip, to everything in the classroom has helped me shape my opinions and the way I think and how I look at things.

Hudson College provided a number of experiences that facilitated Kayla's integration of learning. From the *Liberal Arts Workshop* and *Freshman Symposium* to her coursework and research trip to Tibet, Kayla's experience at Hudson offered excellent examples of institutional practices that promote integration of learning across both in- and out-of-class contexts.

Steve: Reconsidering Religion.   Steve attended Wabash College and was involved in the fraternity community. A common topic through Steve's four-year interview set was religion, in particular the Roman Catholic faith. Steve was raised in a Catholic family, and upon entering college became involved with the local parish and the Newman Club, a Catholic student organization found on many campuses. In his first-year interview, he was assessed with a developmental level of Eb on the self-authorship continuum, indicating tension with trusting external authority. Here, Steve commented on how his religious beliefs connected to his coursework and cocurricular involvement.

> I guess as far as my religious activities, that just kind of gives me a guideline for what I want to do. I don't want to be involved in any human cloning or anything so that's one area of biology that's out, but and as far as with the fraternity, that kind of gives me a guide of how I want to act or what I want to do in certain situations. And as far as looking for what I want to do in biology, the fraternity helps me because there is a lot of guys who have looked into a lot more stuff than I have and they're upper classmen and they can help me and tell me what they're doing to get me prepared not necessarily for what career I want, but how I can find what career I want or something like that I guess.

As a first-year student, Steve easily drew connections between his interest in biology coursework and his involvement with the Newman Club and his fraternity. However, by the next fall, Steve began to question his identity as a Catholic, and was not as certain about connections between faith, his coursework, and career choices. At this point, his developmental level had shifted to E(I), realizing the dilemma of external meaning making.

> As far as the Newman Club, I don't know, I'm still Catholic I guess, (laughs) but I don't know. The more I go to church the less I want to go. I don't know if I'm going to keep going very long so. Yeah, it still feels like there is a God, but I don't know if He really cares if I worship him or not. . . . I go to church once a week and I don't know. Like I still pray before meals and stuff, but I don't know. I think it's more superstition than if I actually believe or not. But I don't know (laughs). But like as far as my actual beliefs though, I just like see how big the universe is and [think about] science. . . matter and mass can't be created or destroyed and energy can't, so I feel like for there to be a beginning. I mean there has to be a beginning, I would think. Yeah, it's a little over my head in understanding, but I just figure there almost has to be. I mean there's definitely something that we don't know like physically that happens or there had to be like a higher being that started it I think, but at the same time like I don't understand why He or She or It would make this huge universe if we were all He cared about. But, I don't know.

Steve continued later in his sophomore interview to describe conversations he had with peers who held different beliefs from those with which he was raised in the Catholic Church.

> There's three Lutheran guys in our [fraternity]. . . . They'd always just start conversations with me about how Catholicism is wrong and then I'd kind of, we'd get ferocious and fight back and forth for a while and it was pretty fun. But yeah, so those [conversations] kind of got me thinking just how humans went from one religion to thousands just within Christianity and it's like how can Catholicism be right? It seemed to mess things up, so I don't know. Oh yeah and then I also took, I completely forgot about this, I took like a Christianity or Hebrew Bible class last year. There's so much stuff that's been translated two or three times at least. Then it's been translated since translat[ion], I know. I just can't imagine everything, like all the church doctrines, no matter what religion, being what God intended, if He did indeed intend anything.

This represented a marked shift for Steve in his view of religion. He was integrating learning, but in a more complex way that allowed him to see a number of critical views from courses and peers alongside his earlier view of the Catholic Church. He appeared to struggle with these new perspectives and continued to go through the motions of attending Mass and praying before meals, even as he questioned his belief structure.

In the summer between his sophomore and junior years, Steve spent a month in Ecuador visiting Quito, the rainforest, and the Galapagos Islands as part of a Wabash College program. As he began his third year in college, his self-authorship level was I(E), nearing the end of the crossroads phase. In the following excerpt from his third-year interview, Steve continued discussing his views on faith, Catholicism, and the existence of God, saying,

> I stopped going to church the beginning of the spring semester of last year so I was pretty into it my whole freshman year, but I don't know. . . . The more I went, the longer I was at Wabash, the more I thought about just important things as opposed to just doing stuff. So the longer I was here the more, they [Wabash] want us to "think critically" [which] is our motto or whatever. So I just started thinking more about stuff, the different things and then listening to my priest, especially my priest back home. I had a lot of contact with him when I was in high school, just the more I thought about some of the stuff that he would tell me it just seemed more like propaganda than anything. And then also I've taken a few classes about like the history of the church and it just seemed like it was so corrupt back in the day, I just don't see how you could salvage a church that was so corrupt to make it something good. . . . So I figure I can be a good person, maybe even a better person, without church. I don't feel I need the church to tell me to be a good person to help people in need so I feel like it's a waste of money and time to go to church. . . . I try to think a lot and talk to a lot of people about whether or not God exists. Not that anyone would really know, but just to make a decision for myself what I believe because I really don't know what I believe right now, but I know that or I believe that if God does exist, the Catholic Church is not what He wants (laughs). So I hope you're not Catholic or anything. [Interviewer: Oh yeah, I am Catholic.] Oh sorry, but that's just my personal feeling. [I: But I take no offense.] Okay, cool.

This excerpt illustrates the growing complexity in Steve's integration of learning. He drew on his courses in church history, and also invoked Wabash's mission to educate men "to think critically, act responsibly, lead effectively, and live humanely" as he considered his view of Catholicism. He was confident in his opinion, and comfortable expressing a perspective differing from that of the interviewer.

By the time Steve had his fourth interview, he no longer considered himself Catholic. At this point in time, he was entering self-authorship, with a developmental level of Ia, indicating a trust in his own internal voice. In the following excerpt, Steve reflected back on the evolution of his view on faith over his time as a college student.

> I took a course about some of the corruption of the church in the Middle Ages, and just the more I looked into these things, I was like, maybe these aren't in place for spiritual reasons, but more for just to control people and get them to pay money. . . . Even bringing it up with my parents and other people, just nothing really brought me back and made me want to do it anymore. It

kind of sucks because I go to church with my parents, with my mom, just
something to do with them and I mean, I kind of wish I believed it, I guess,
because, it was pretty nice [to] believe you're going to go somewhere after
you die and—but, for me, sometimes I wish I did but at the same time, I
don't want to. Why believe that I'm lying to myself and just go to church just
in case? If I'm going to go, I actually want to believe in the things I'm believing
in. Does that make sense?

In this excerpt, Steve synthesized a new view of religion and spiritual-
ity for himself, drawing from his experiences with his home parish priest,
new college priest, his course on church corruption, and his exposure to
nonreligious peers. He combines elements learned from each venue, combining these into a new agnostic worldview (even though he in some ways
mourns this loss of faith).

Discussion

Although it is difficult to fully illustrate the scope of the longitudinal
data from three students' interview sets in a single chapter, the examples provided here from Reese, Kayla, and Steve demonstrate that students
have a greater capacity to integrate learning as they progress through college and develop a more internal self-authorship orientation. Curricular
and cocurricular programs (including study abroad, discussion-based academic courses, undergraduate research opportunities, and conversations
with peers in student residences) played a key role in fostering these abilities. As such, the faculty, staff, and administrators who direct these initiatives have both an opportunity and a responsibility to guide student learning
and development.

Qualitative research methods are strong tools for examining the complexities of student learning and meaning making. The examples in this
chapter also highlight the value of studying the entire four-year interview
set for an individual student, and the impact that this format can have
for research-driven practice in student affairs. Investigating each year's interview separately provides discrete data about personal development and
learning, but greater depth and intricacy is possible when analyzing the
student's full college story. For example, in Reese's case, her experiences at
summer camp, mentioned briefly in her freshman year, eventually are revealed to serve an essential role in integrating learning across contexts, influencing her experiences with career choice, interpersonal relationships,
study abroad, and foreign language classes. Student affairs professionals
often have the opportunity to work with individual students over several
years, allowing for an opportunity to recognize ongoing developmental sto-
rylines, understand a student's personal background and family context,
and promote the integration of learning.

New Directions for Student Services • DOI: 10.1002/ss

Implications for Research-Driven Practice

The student interview sets explored in this chapter also raise a number of implications for educational practice for faculty and administrators alike. In seeking to promote integration of learning among students, I offer the following recommendations for college educators.

Study Away.   Examples from these three students support the notion that study abroad experiences can promote integration of learning by introducing multiple perspectives. All three of the students featured in this analysis participated in a formalized study abroad program. In the 2011–2012 academic year, just over 9% of U.S. undergraduates took part in a study abroad experience (Institute of International Education, 2013). Sobania and Braskamp (2009) suggest that cross-cultural study domestically (i.e., "study away") can be effective in introducing multiple perspectives as well. Student affairs professionals should work with faculty and administrators to make such programs accessible to more students, both in terms of finances and scheduling.

Engage With Diverse Others.   Student experiences shared in this chapter indicate that diverse peers provide a context to evaluate one's own beliefs and struggle to integrate the new perspectives with existing beliefs. Steve's recollection of his "ferocious" yet "fun" debates with his Lutheran fraternity brothers illustrates this point, and the importance of a diverse campus community for fostering integration of learning both in and out of class. This underscores the importance of developing the structural diversity of our campus community in terms of visible difference such as race, ethnicity, and national origin, as well as less visible forms of diversity like sexual orientation, faith, politics, and socioeconomic status.

In terms of research-driven practice, student affairs professionals must continue to strive for increasing diversity in all aspects of campus life. Although structural diversity is not always within the control of student affairs professionals, interactional diversity, cocurricular diversity, and curricular diversity (Hurtado, Milem, Clayton-Pedersen, & Allen, 1999) are areas in which student affairs departments, including residence life, fraternity/sorority affairs, first-year experience, and campus recreation, can make substantive contributions.

Prioritize Mentoring in Education.   Several of the students in this analysis described the importance of class discussions and faculty-led programs to their learning; however, the majority of these interactions were short-lived. By contrast, Kayla's interviews provide excellent examples of the power of an ongoing faculty partner in advancing student development and creating opportunities for integration of learning. In addition, the longitudinal approach to this analysis illustrates the importance of a consistent mentor throughout the college experience; one can grasp a much more complete picture of student learning when engaged with the student's interview set spanning four years.

Frankly, the lack of such sustained relationships is distressing. The absence of substantive and ongoing guidance or partnership for students in this analysis (as well as in the larger WNS data) indicates a need to prioritize mentoring in our work as educators. Student affairs professionals are well-positioned to heed this call, and utilize the resources of campus networks and professional associations to encourage faculty, staff, and alumni to place a greater emphasis on student mentoring. As students encounter new knowledge, diverse peers, and different perspectives that may conflict with their existing beliefs, worldviews may be disrupted. In Steve's words, such new learning can "mess things up." College educators possess the skills and expertise to help students process multiple points of view, as well as work through the discomfort of dissonance rather than dismissing it, and ultimately integrate learning.

Conclusion

Integration of learning is an essential educational outcome for U.S. college and university students in the 21st century. This chapter provides empirical data on the process of integrating learning for college students in an effort to uncover patterns in the development of integration of learning over a four-year undergraduate career.

My research with the WNS (building on my experience as a student affairs professional) has confirmed for me that the analysis of a student's four-year interview set is a powerful approach that provides a wider lens to study how college students learn and develop over time, while allowing for a substantial investigation of a contextualized experience. Student affairs professionals can use this research to support their practice and prioritize how best to spend precious time and resources to best support student learning. In building on the established developmental framework of self-authorship, this research also contributes to the data describing the journey from an externally defined point of view to a perspective that is increasingly internally conceived. Lastly, this approach capitalizes on a unique opportunity for analysis of longitudinal qualitative data.

Note

1. All student names are pseudonyms.

References

AAC&U. (2002). *Greater expectations: A new vision for learning as a nation goes to college*. Retrieved from http://www.greaterexpectations.org/

AAC&U & Carnegie Foundation. (2004). *A statement on integrative learning*. Washington, DC: Authors.

ACPA. (1994). *The student learning imperative*. Washington, DC: ACPA-College Student Educators International.

Barber, J. P. (2009). *Integration of learning: Meaning making for undergraduates through connection, application, and synthesis* (Doctoral dissertation). University of Michigan, Ann Arbor. (UMI No. 3354010)

Barber, J. P. (2012). Integration of learning: A grounded theory of college students' learning. *American Educational Research Journal, 49*(3), 590–617. doi:10.3102/0002831212437854

Barber, J. P. (2014). Integration of learning model: How college students integrate learning. In P. Eddy (Ed.), *New Directions for Higher Education: No. 165. Connecting learning across the institution* (pp. 7–17). San Francisco, CA: Jossey-Bass. doi:10.1002/he.20079

Barber, J. P., & King, P. M. (2014). Pathways toward self-authorship: Student responses to the demands of developmentally effective experiences. *Journal of College Student Development, 55*(5), 433–450.

Barber, J. P., King, P. M., & Baxter Magolda, M. B. (2013). Long strides on the journey toward self-authorship: Substantial developmental shifts in college students' meaning making. *Journal of Higher Education, 84*(6), 866–896. doi:10.1353/jhe.2013.0033

Baxter Magolda, M. B. (1998). Developing self-authorship in young adult life. *Journal of College Student Development, 39*(2), 143–156.

Baxter Magolda, M. B. (1999). *Creating contexts for learning and self-authorship: Constructive-developmental pedagogy.* Nashville, TN: Vanderbilt University Press.

Baxter Magolda, M. B. (2001). *Making their own way: Narratives for transforming higher education to promote self-development.* Sterling, VA: Stylus.

Baxter Magolda, M. B. (2009). *Authoring your life: Developing an internal voice to navigate life's challenges.* Sterling, VA: Stylus.

Baxter Magolda, M. B., & King, P. M. (2012). *Assessing meaning making and self-authorship: Theory, research, and application* [ASHE Higher Education Report Series, 38(3)]. San Francisco, CA: Jossey-Bass. doi:10.1002/aehe.20003

Charmaz, K. (2006). *Constructing grounded theory: A practical guide through qualitative analysis.* Thousand Oaks, CA: Sage.

Glaser, B. G., & Strauss, A. L. (1967). *The discovery of grounded theory: Strategies for qualitative research.* Chicago, IL: Aldine.

Hurtado, S., Milem, J. F., Clayton-Pedersen, A. R., & Allen, W. R. (1999). *Enacting diverse learning environments: Improving the climate for racial/ethnic diversity in higher education institutions* [ASHE-ERIC Higher Education Report, 26(8)]. Washington, DC: George Washington University.

Institute of International Education. (2013). *Open doors 2013 fast facts.* Retrieved from http://www.iie.org/~/media/Files/Corporate/Open-Doors/Fast-Facts/Fast-Facts-2013.ashx

Joint Task Force on Student Learning. (1998). *Powerful partnerships: A shared responsibility for learning.* Retrieved from http://www.acpa.nche.edu/powerful-partnerships-shared-responsibility-learning

Keeling, R. P. (Ed.). (2004). *Learning reconsidered: A campus-wide focus on the student experience.* Washington, DC: NASPA & ACPA.

Kegan, R. (1994). *In over our heads: The mental demands of modern life.* Cambridge, MA: Harvard University Press.

King, P. M., Baxter Magolda, M. B., Barber, J. P., Kendall Brown, M., & Lindsay, N. K. (2009). Developmentally effective experiences for promoting self-authorship. *Mind, Brain, and Education, 3*(2), 106–116. doi:10.1111/j.1751-228X.2009.01061.x

King, P. M., Kendall Brown, M., Lindsay, N. K., & VanHecke, J. R. (2007). Liberal arts student learning outcomes: An integrated perspective. *About Campus, 12*(4), 2–9. doi:10.1002/abc.222

Lincoln, Y. S., & Guba, E. G. (1985). *Naturalistic inquiry.* Thousand Oaks, CA: Sage.

Sobania, N., & Braskamp, L. A. (2009). Study abroad or study away: It's not merely semantics. *Peer Review, 11*(4), 23–26.

Strauss, A., & Corbin, J. (1998). *Basics of qualitative research: Techniques and procedures for developing grounded theory.* Thousand Oaks, CA: Sage.

JAMES P. BARBER is an assistant professor of education at the College of William & Mary.

7

This chapter surveys WNS findings that explored how "at-risk" identities affect students' educational outcomes and offers advice on how to ensure the success of these students.

What the Wabash National Study Can Teach Us About At-Risk Student Populations

Teniell L. Trolian

"At-risk" students have been defined in a number of ways in the postsecondary education literature. Identifying students to be at-risk stems from definitions of students who have been shown to be at risk of dropping out of school in K–12 education (Horn & Carroll, 1997). In the K–12 context, students who have been identified as most at-risk are those who come from the lowest socioeconomic groups, come from single-parent families, have siblings who have dropped out of school, frequently change schools, have lower grade point averages, or have repeated a grade during their schooling (Horn, Chen, & Adelman, 1998). Quinnan (1997) observed, "'At-risk' suggests students who are in danger of failing to pass required courses and navigate the prescribed curriculum ... class and culture biases replete in the schooling process have been raised as factors contributing to the 'at-risk' equation" (p. 30).

Borrowing from the K–12 literature on at-risk students, postsecondary education researchers, administrators, and policy makers have revised the definition of at-risk students to include students who are at risk of not attending college (Choy, Horn, Nuñez, & Chen, 2000), those who attend but struggle to be successful (Pizzolato, 2003), and those who attend but are less likely to graduate (Reason, 2009). According to Pizzolato (2003), "researchers conceptualize the high-risk [or at-risk] college student as one whose academic background (academic preparation), prior performance (low high school or first-semester college GPA), or personal characteristics may contribute to academic failure or early withdrawal from college" (p. 798). Similarly, studies of at-risk college students have defined the term "at-risk" in a number of contexts. Some studies have focused exclusively on those students who are academically at-risk (e.g., Levin & Levin, 1991),

NEW DIRECTIONS FOR STUDENT SERVICES, no. 147, Fall 2014 © 2014 Wiley Periodicals, Inc.
Published online in Wiley Online Library (wileyonlinelibrary.com) • DOI: 10.1002/ss.20102

while others have emphasized at-risk factors such as student background characteristics (e.g., Yeh, 2002).

Further, it seems that the definition of at-risk students in postsecondary education is continually developing as understandings of college students and institutions expand. Bulger and Watson (2006) argued that the definition of at-risk student should be revised to include a combination of student background characteristics (e.g., age, socioeconomic status, disability status), internal characteristics (e.g., self-concept), and environmental factors (e.g., access to support and resources) that take into account the context in which postsecondary students live today. According to Swail (2009):

> There are a number of social factors that may impact a student's ability to persist and ultimately attain a postsecondary degree. These include delayed enrollment (from high school to postsecondary school), not having a high school diploma, enrolling part-time rather than full-time, being financially independent, having dependent children, being a single parent, and working full-time while enrolled.... In general, the more risk characteristics a student has, the greater the chance that he or she will not complete college. (p. 14)

The literature on postsecondary education has typically used the following characteristics in identifying students who may be at-risk: first-generation students, students from lower socioeconomic backgrounds, racial/ethnic minority students, adult or returning students, academically underprepared students, and students with disabilities. These characteristics have been highlighted throughout the research literature on at-risk students, and they have been studied by researchers using data from the Wabash National Study of Liberal Arts Education (WNS). This chapter provides an overview of WNS studies that have examined the college experiences and outcomes of at-risk students and how these findings may have implications for higher education and student affairs professionals.

Wabash National Study and At-Risk Student Populations

Research from the Wabash National Study has examined the effects of college and college experiences on intended outcomes of postsecondary education. Early studies from the WNS focused on outcomes of the first year of postsecondary education, while research that is more recent has examined outcomes over four years of college. Further, a number of studies have used data from the Wabash National Study to understand the experiences of at-risk students. While some researchers have examined the experiences of at-risk students as a central research question, others have looked at general effects for students overall and conditional effects for students with at-risk characteristics. WNS research on at-risk students has attempted to identify the effects of academic experiences, experiences with diversity, and out-of-class experiences on college outcomes. This section will explore the research on the effects of college and college experiences on the intended outcomes of college for at-risk student populations.

Academic Experiences.   Research from the Wabash National Study has investigated the effects of a number of academic experiences on student outcomes during college. One study explored the relationship between institutional type and exposure to good practices during the first year of college (Seifert, Pascarella, Goodman, Salisbury, & Blaich, 2010). Results indicated that students who attended a liberal arts college reported more exposure to good teaching, high-quality faculty interactions, and high levels of academic rigor than students at other types of institutions. The authors also explored a number of conditional effects, finding that attendance at a liberal arts college "tended to foster the greatest impact on engagement in, or exposure to good practices for students who entered postsecondary education with lower levels of tested precollege academic preparation, precollege academic motivation, high school involvement, or family educational background" (p. 15). These results suggest that attending a liberal arts college may allow at-risk students to derive additional benefit from higher education in terms of having exposure to vetted good practices during the first year of college.

Another study investigated the effects of high-impact/good practices on end-of-fourth-year critical thinking, need for cognition, and positive attitudes toward literacy (Seifert, Gillig, Hanson, Pascarella, & Blaich, 2014). Findings revealed that several high-impact/good practices had a positive influence on all three dependent measures, including interactional diversity, which had a significant positive influence on all three outcomes, and working with a faculty member on a research project, which had a significant positive influence on need for cognition and positive attitudes toward literacy. However, the major contribution of this study was in its evaluation of conditional effects for students with differing background characteristics. Conditional analyses revealed that students' precollege critical thinking scores moderated the effect of interactions with faculty and student affairs staff on fourth-year critical thinking, suggesting that the effect of interactions with faculty and student affairs staff was more positive for students with higher precollege critical thinking scores than for students with lower precollege critical thinking scores. Similarly, results indicated that students with higher precollege positive attitudes toward literacy scores derived greater benefits, in terms of fourth-year positive attitudes toward literacy, from their interactions with faculty and student affairs staff. These results again suggest that students' background characteristics and precollege cognitive ability have an influence on their overall college experiences and outcomes.

Research using the WNS has also considered the effects of at-risk student background characteristics, specifically first-generation student status, on a number of college outcomes. Results from a study examining the effects of first-generation student status on a number of college outcomes (Padgett, Johnson, & Pascarella, 2012) suggested that first-generation students were at a significant disadvantage in terms of their gains in attitudes toward literacy, intercultural effectiveness and universal-diverse orientation, and psychological well-being during the first year of college. Further, the effects of good practice differed for first-generation and continuing-generation students. Specifically, first-generation students derived greater psychosocial and cognitive benefits during the first year of college from interactions with peers and from exposure to academically challenging experiences, while interactions with faculty negatively influenced several measures of psychosocial and cognitive development for first-generation students. These results suggest that first-generation students, who are often considered at-risk, may be at a disadvantage in terms of their cognitive and psychosocial development during college when compared to their continuing-generation peers.

Two studies using data from the first year of the Wabash National Study also examined student aspirations to study abroad during college. One of these projects explored the effects of socioeconomic status on students' aspirations to study abroad using an applied college choice model. The authors noted, "An integrated model of student choice, already successfully applied to decisions of enrollment and persistence, may provide insights into a range of student decisions regarding participation in meaningful educational activities during the college experience" (Salisbury, Umbach, Paulsen, & Pascarella, 2009, p. 137). Results of the study indicated that students who had received federal financial aid were less likely to study abroad than those who had not received federal financial aid. Similarly, students whose parents had lower levels of formal education were less likely to study abroad than those whose parents had higher levels of formal education. These results suggest that students from at-risk socioeconomic backgrounds may be less likely to study abroad and, as a consequence, may be less likely to derive benefits associated with study abroad experiences during college.

Another study interested in student aspirations to study abroad during college looked at differences between White, African-American, Hispanic, and Asian-American students' aspirations using first-year data across all three cohorts of the Wabash National Study (Salisbury, Paulsen, & Pascarella, 2011). The effects of other factors on students' intent to study abroad, such as socioeconomic status, precollege ability, parental education, and receipt of a federal grant, varied greatly for students from minority racial/ethnic backgrounds. White students with higher socioeconomic status and with higher levels of social and cultural capital were more likely to study abroad than non-White students. African-American students with higher precollege ability (as measured by students' ACT or equivalent score) were less likely to study abroad than other students. However, if African-American students entered college with high levels of social and cultural capital, they were more likely to study abroad. For Asian-American students, higher levels of parental education decreased the odds of studying abroad, while higher levels of social and cultural capital made Asian-American students more likely to study abroad. Finally, Hispanic students who received a federal grant during their first year of college and with higher levels of social and cultural capital were more likely to study abroad. These results suggest that possessing social and cultural capital mattered across racial/ethnic groups, where higher levels of social and cultural capital were associated with students' intent to study abroad.

Experiences With Diversity.   Several studies have also examined experiences with diversity during the first year of college for at-risk students. One project sought to understand the effects of first-year exposure to classroom and interactional diversity experiences on social and political activism (Pascarella, Salisbury, Martin, & Blaich, 2012). Findings suggested that exposure to interactional diversity contributed to students' overall attitudes about the importance of social and political activism and their orientation toward liberal political views, and classroom diversity had a small positive effect on social and political activism. However, the direction and magnitude of this effect differed for students across background characteristics. First, the effect of interactional diversity on liberal political views was moderated by sex, where male students were more likely to have made shifts toward liberal political views than female students. Second, the effect of interactional diversity on liberal political views for students with ACT scores of 24 or lower was more than 10 times larger than students with ACT scores of 29 or higher and twice as large as students with ACT scores between 25 and 28. That is, students with lower ACT scores were more likely to have made shifts toward liberal political views than students with higher ACT scores. These results provide evidence that students who are often considered at-risk may be affected differently by the same experiences at college.

In another study of diversity experiences, researchers considered the effect of students' experiences with diversity in the first year of college on critical thinking skills (Loes, Pascarella, & Umbach, 2012). While results showed there was no general effect of diversity experiences on first-year critical thinking skills, results of conditional analyses revealed that the effect of interactional diversity on critical thinking at the end of the first year of college differed for students based on their precollege academic ability. For students in the sample with lower precollege academic ability, interactional diversity had a significant positive effect on critical thinking, but for students with higher precollege academic ability, interactional diversity had little effect on critical thinking. Results of conditional analyses also revealed that interactional diversity had a significant positive effect on first-year critical thinking for White students, but had no significant effect on critical thinking for Students of Color. These results suggest that exposure to diversity in college may affect at-risk students in different ways, influencing students with lower levels of precollege academic ability positively, but having little influence on students from racial/ethnic minority backgrounds.

A follow-up to this first-year study examined the effects of interactional diversity experiences on fourth-year critical thinking skills (Pascarella et al., 2014), finding that interactional diversity had a significant and positive general effect on critical thinking skills at the end of the fourth year of college. However, additional analyses revealed that interactional diversity experiences had a stronger positive effect on four-year critical thinking for students with lower levels of precollege ability than for students with higher levels. These results suggest that exposure to interactional diversity experiences may actually have a strong positive effect on four-year critical thinking gains for students whose academic ability may place them at-risk.

Students' at-risk identities have also been shown to influence cognitive gains from enrolling in diversity courses during the first year of college. One study revealed that students who had taken at least one diversity course during college had significantly higher gains in need for cognition (Bowman, 2009). Additionally, students from low- or middle-income backgrounds benefited more from taking a diversity course than did high-income students, and White students benefited more than Students of Color from taking a diversity course. These results suggest that at-risk factors, such as race and socioeconomic status, may influence students' gains in need for cognition, at least in the first year of college.

Out-of-Class Experiences.   A number of studies have used data from the WNS to explore in- and out-of-class experiences for at-risk students during the first year of college. One study examined the effects of socialization on students' need for cognition, considering the effect of three primary socialization factors: quality of nonclassroom interactions with faculty, co-operative learning, and meaningful discussions with diverse peers (Padgett et al., 2010). Results suggested that participation in quality nonclassroom interactions with faculty and meaningful discussions with diverse peers were positively associated with overall student gains in need for cognition. Further, results indicated that Asian/Pacific Islander students reported lower gains in need for cognition as compared to White students, and first-generation students' participation in nonclassroom interactions with faculty actually had a negative effect on their reported need for cognition scores. These findings suggest that while participation in quality nonclassroom interactions with faculty and meaningful discussions with diverse peers may have overall positive effects for students, the results may be conditional for students with at-risk background factors.

Researchers have also investigated the effects of student employment on the development of leadership skills during the first year of college (Salisbury, Pascarella, Padgett, & Blaich, 2012). Specifically, they sought to determine whether on- and off-campus work at varying degrees of frequency had an effect on students' first-year leadership development, as measured by the Socially Responsible Leadership Scale. Results of the study revealed that working more than 10 hours per week during the first year of college had a significant and positive effect on leadership development, and off-campus work had a stronger positive effect than on-campus work. However, the authors noted, "While working more than 10 hours per week positively affected leadership development, extensive work off-campus simultaneously limited peer interaction and co-curricular involvement—activities that also enhance leadership skills" (p. 318). As students from lower socioeconomic backgrounds and students from non-White and non-Asian racial groups are more likely to work more hours per week during college (King, 2006), these results suggest that working students, many of whom may be low-income or racial/ethnic minority students, may derive some benefit in terms of their leadership development.

Research has also examined the effects of fraternity/sorority member-ship on several liberal arts educational outcomes: critical thinking, moral reasoning, inclination to inquire and lifelong learning (as measured by need for cognition and attitudes toward literacy activities), and psycho-logical well-being (Hevel, Martin, Weeden, & Pascarella, in press; Martin, Hevel, Asel, & Pascarella, 2011). While no significant net effects of frater-nity/sorority membership were found for any of the measured liberal arts outcomes, several conditional effects were revealed in the authors' anal-yses. Race was a significant moderator of the effect of fraternity/sorority membership on moral reasoning development over four years of college, where White students had a statistically significant advantage in moral rea-soning growth, while Students of Color had a significant disadvantage. Sim-ilarly, race was a moderator of the effect of fraternity/sorority membership on growth in critical thinking skills; White students had a significant dis-advantage in critical thinking growth, while Students of Color had a pos-itive but nonsignificant advantage in critical thinking. Conditional effects were also found for students who entered college with lower levels of crit-ical thinking and need for cognition. Fraternity/sorority members whose precollege critical thinking scores were in the lower two thirds of the dis-tribution had a significant disadvantage in critical thinking skills after four years of college, when compared to their nonaffiliated peers. Similarly, fra-ternity/sorority members who entered college in the highest one third of the need for cognition distribution had a significant advantage in terms of need for cognition. Again, student background characteristics that may place stu-dents at-risk, such as racial/ethnic minority status and precollege academic ability, were found to influence college outcomes.

Discussion and Recommendations for Student Affairs Practice

Overall, results from the Wabash National Study suggest that, in terms of college outcomes, who you are matters. College experiences and outcomes appear to differ for at-risk students when compared to students who do not possess any of the identified at-risk characteristics (e.g., first-generation stu-dents, students from lower socioeconomic backgrounds, racial/ethnic mi-nority students, adult or returning students, academically underprepared students, students with disabilities). In several studies, students with one or more at-risk characteristics were more or less likely to engage in certain behaviors during college or were more or less likely to derive benefits from college and university good practices or experiences.

Further, studies using data from the Wabash National Study also highlighted the potential compensatory effects of postsecondary education for students who may be at-risk. In some studies, at-risk students reported higher gains in some cognitive and psychosocial outcomes over time. These findings suggest that at-risk students may derive significant benefits that may actually compensate for background characteristics that place them at-risk when entering college. This is an important finding for higher education and students affairs professionals interested in issues of access and persistence, as this suggests that at-risk student populations may stand to gain the most from successfully earning a college degree.

Evidence from this body of research has several implications for higher education and student affairs professionals interested in supporting the success and persistence of at-risk students. Professionals must consider that at-risk students may experience postsecondary education differently and reflect on the ways in which these experiences may affect at-risk students' learning and development. Colleges and universities continue to enroll significantly larger populations of students, which can often lead higher education and student affairs professionals to adopt a "one-size-fits-all" approach to student learning and development. In using these approaches, the unique needs of at-risk students may be overlooked, and professionals must rethink their work with students in order to better support the success and attainment of at-risk students.

Colleges and universities should develop strategies to identify at-risk students in order to appropriately intervene and provide necessary resources to support student success. In considering student success in college, Kuh, Kinzie, Buckley, Bridges, and Hayek (2007) noted, "Most students, especially those who start college with two or more characteristics associated with early departure, benefit from early interventions and sustained attention at various transition points in their educational journey" (p. ix). Resources such as supplemental instruction, tutoring, writing support, psychological counseling, or educational and social programming have the potential to positively influence the success and persistence of at-risk students, and early intervention may help to mediate potential for academic failure or early departure.

Identifying and supporting students with at-risk characteristics will require new and strengthened partnerships across college and university campuses. Providing assistance to at-risk students will require ongoing communication and collaboration between college faculty, staff, and administrators. As at-risk students attempt to navigate admission, financial aid, residential living, student involvement, career planning, and academic services (to name a few), academic affairs and student affairs professionals will need to work cooperatively to ensure that students maximize use of these and other important campus resources.

NEW DIRECTIONS FOR STUDENT SERVICES • DOI: 10.1002/ss

Finally, findings from the Wabash National Study suggest that colleges and universities ought to consider ways to continue to promote student exposure to diversity during college. Exposure to interactional diversity and diversity experiences has been shown to contribute to gains in critical thinking skills and to positive student attitudes about the importance of being socially and politically involved, and these gains have been shown to be more pronounced for students with lower levels of academic ability. In this sense, increased exposure to diversity in college may help at-risk students to derive compensatory benefits from the college experience.

Conclusion

There is a lot to be learned from the Wabash National Study of Liberal Arts Education, particularly as it relates to at-risk student populations. While research using the WNS has focused on the experiences of some at-risk students (such as those with lower precollege academic ability, first-generation students, students from lower socioeconomic backgrounds, and those from racial/ethnic minority backgrounds), additional research is needed to better understand the college experiences and outcomes of at-risk students. Future research that explores the experiences of adult or returning students or students with disabilities may be a good place to begin, as well as future research that investigates the experiences of students with more than one risk factor.

References

Bowman, N. A. (2009). College diversity courses and cognitive development among students from privileged and marginalized groups. *Journal of Diversity in Higher Education*, 2(3), 182–194. doi:10.1037/a0016639

Bulger, S., & Watson, D. (2006). Broadening the definition of at-risk students. *Community College Enterprise*, 12(2), 23–32.

Choy, S. P., Horn, L. J., Nuñez, A. M., & Chen, X. (2000). Transition to college: What helps at-risk students and students whose parents did not attend college. In A. F. Cabrera & S. M. La Nasa (Eds.), *New Directions for Institutional Research: No. 107. Understanding the college choice of disadvantaged students* (pp. 45–63). San Francisco, CA: Jossey-Bass.

Hevel, M. S., Martin, G. L., Weeden, D. D., & Pascarella, E. T. (in press). The effects of fraternity and sorority membership in the fourth year of college: A detrimental or value-added component of undergraduate education? *Journal of College Student Development*.

Horn, L. J., & Carroll, C. D. (1997). *Confronting the odds: Students at risk and the pipeline to higher education* (Report No. NCES 98-094). National Center for Education Statistics. Washington, DC: U.S. Department of Education, Office of Educational Research and Improvement.

Horn, L. J., Chen, X., & Adelman, C. (1998). *Toward resiliency: At-risk students who make it to college*. Washington, DC: U.S. Department of Education, Office of Educational Research and Improvement.

King, J. (2006). Working their way through college: Student employment and its impact on the college experience. *American Council on Education Issue Brief.* Retrieved from http://www.acenet.edu/news-room/Documents/IssueBrief-2006-Working-their-way -through-College.pdf

Kuh, G. D., Kinzie, J., Buckley, J. A., Bridges, B. K., & Hayek, J. C. (2007). *Piecing together the student success puzzle: Research, propositions, and recommendations* [ASHE Higher Education Report, 32(5)]. Washington, DC: Graduate School of Education and Human Development, The George Washington University.

Levin, M. E., & Levin, J. R. (1991). A critical examination of academic retention programs for at-risk minority college students. *Journal of College Student Development, 32,* 323–334.

Loes, C., Pascarella, E. T., & Umbach, P. D. (2012). Effects of diversity experiences on critical thinking skills: Who benefits? *Journal of Higher Education, 83,* 1–25. doi:10.1353/jhe.2012.0001

Martin, G. L., Hevel, M. S., Asel, A. M., & Pascarella, E. T. (2011). New evidence of the effect of fraternity and sorority affiliation during the first year of college. *Journal of College Student Development, 52,* 543–559. doi:10.1353/csd.2011.0062

Padgett, R. D., Goodman, K. M., Johnson, M. P., Saichaie, K., Umbach, P. D., & Pascarella, E. T. (2010). The impact of college student socialization, social class, and race on need for cognition. In S. Herzog (Ed.), *New Directions for Institutional Research: No. 145. Diversity and education benefits* (pp. 99–111). San Francisco, CA: Jossey-Bass.

Padgett, R. D., Johnson, M. P., & Pascarella, E. T. (2012). First-generation undergraduate students and the impacts of the first year of college: Additional evidence. *Journal of College Student Development, 53,* 243–266. doi:10.1353/csd.2012.0032

Pascarella, E. T., Martin, G. L., Hanson, J. M., Trolian, T. L., Gillig, B., & Blaich, C. (2014). Effects of diversity experiences on critical thinking skills over four years of college. *Journal of College Student Development, 55,* 86–92. doi:10.1353/csd.2014.0009

Pascarella, E. T., Salisbury, M. H., Martin, G. L., & Blaich, C. (2012). Some complexities in the effects of diversity experiences on orientation toward social/political activism and political views in the first year of college. *The Journal of Higher Education, 83,* 467–496. doi:10.1353/jhe.2012.0026

Pizzolato, J. E. (2003). Developing self-authorship: Exploring the experiences of high-risk college students. *Journal of College Student Development, 44,* 797–812. doi:10.1353/csd.2003.0074

Quinnan, T. W. (1997). Adult students "at-risk": Theoretical definitions. In H. A. Ciroux & P. Fiere (Eds.), *Adult students at-risk: Culture bias in higher education* (Critical Studies in Education Series; pp. 27–44). Westport, CT: Bergin & Garvey.

Reason, R. D. (2009). An examination of persistence research through the lens of comprehensive conceptual framework. *Journal of College Student Development, 50,* 659–682. doi:10.1353/csd.0.0098

Salisbury, M. H., Pascarella, E. T., Padgett, R. D., & Blaich, C. (2012). The effects of work on leadership development among first-year college students. *Journal of College Student Development, 53,* 300–324. doi:10.1353/csd.2012.0021

Salisbury, M. H., Paulsen, M. B., & Pascarella, E. T. (2011). Why do all the study abroad students look alike? Applying an integrated student choice model to explore differences in the factors that influence White and minority students' intent to study abroad. *Research in Higher Education, 52,* 123–150. doi:10.1007/s11162-010-9191-2

Salisbury, M. H., Umbach, P. D., Paulsen, M. B., & Pascarella, E. T. (2009). Going global: Understanding the choice process of the intent to study abroad. *Research in Higher Education, 50,* 119–143. doi:10.1007/s11162-008-9111-x

Seifert, T. A., Gillig, B., Hanson, J. M., Pascarella, E. T., & Blaich, C. (2014). The conditional nature of high impact/good practices on student learning outcomes. *The Journal of Higher Education, 85*(4), 531–564. doi:10.1353/jhe.2014.0019

Seifert, T. A., Pascarella, E. T., Goodman, K. M., Salisbury, M. H., & Blaich, C. F. (2010). Liberal arts colleges and good practices in undergraduate education: Additional evidence. *Journal of College Student Development, 51*, 1–22. doi:10.1353/csd.0.0113

Swail, W. S. (2009). Graduating at-risk students: A cross-sector analysis. *Imagining America Foundation.* Retrieved from http://www.imagine-america.org/pdfs/Graduating -At-Risk-Students-Web.pdf

Yeh, T. L. (2002). Asian American college students who are educationally at risk. In M. K. McEwen, C. M. Kodama, A. N. Alvarez, S. Lee, & C. T. H. Liang (Eds.), *New Directions for Student Services: No. 97. Working with Asian American college students* (pp. 61–71). San Francisco, CA: Jossey-Bass.

TENIELL L. TROLIAN *is a doctoral candidate in the Higher Education and Student Affairs Program at the University of Iowa.*

8

This chapter explores the meanings of "scholar-practitioner" and explores habits of mind that encourage participation in scholarly activities and incorporating evidence in professional practice.

Becoming a Scholar-Practitioner in Student Affairs

V. Leilani Kupo

The previous chapters in this volume highlight key findings from the Wabash National Study (WNS) with implications for student affairs professionals. The findings explored are fascinating and have critical implications to the work we do as student affairs practitioners. As I reflect on these findings, I grapple with what to do with this information. Research is a key element in justifying the importance of student affairs work and describing its impact on students' educational outcomes. As a practitioner, I have to think about how I can translate the WNS findings in a manner that is meaningful to campus decision makers and find ways to use it to inform my daily practice. Though this is part of the work, these exercises can be difficult and exhausting. In this chapter, I explore my own process of using research to inform practice with a particular emphasis on how I, and others, can use findings from studies like the WNS to inform and strengthen practice.

Defining "Scholar-Practitioner"

"Theory to practice." "Practice informed by evidence." "What does the literature say?" These phrases echo in my mind as I engage in daily work. I hear the voices of peers, faculty, supervisors, and mentors constantly emphasizing the importance of theory-informed practice. These questions are constant reminders of how I engage in daily reflective practice and serve to center the value of scholarship in my own professional practice. This value frames the choices I make and guides my approach to the work I do in student affairs as a scholar-practitioner. Over the past few years I have been privileged enough to be included in conversations about the role of a scholar-practitioner. The work is based on a framework of values, habits of mind, and the ability to balance and integrate "doing" with "knowing."

New Directions for Student Services, no. 147, Fall 2014 © 2014 Wiley Periodicals, Inc.
Published online in Wiley Online Library (wileyonlinelibrary.com) • DOI: 10.1002/ss.20103

Becoming a scholar-practitioner is not an easy task. However, it is a critical practice to work toward.

In order to be able to engage in the conversation of what defines a scholar-practitioner, it is important to consider what defines scholarship. Scholarship includes original research meant for publication. However, it also includes engaging in research to improve effectiveness of practices. Scholarship can include reviewing current practices and literature, designing assessment plans, benchmarking, participating in self-studies, and so forth. Scholarship also takes the shape of formal presentations at national or regional conferences or presenting evidence to peers at your local university. It is critical to understand the breadth and depth of scholarship within professional practice. A question to ask yourself is "What do you currently do as a scholar-practitioner?" This is an opportunity for self-reflection. Taking time to examine how you are integrating scholarship in daily practice is a good starting point. Exploring one's practice, asking critical questions, and investigating how one utilizes scholarship in daily practice are ways to understand the starting point and how to move forward in one's goals toward becoming a scholar-practitioner.

In many student affairs graduate programs, students are encouraged to ensure that practice is informed by research and grounded in theory. "Student affairs professionals, the faculty who prepare them in graduate programs, and professional associations all play a role in ensuring adequate understanding of relevant research in the field" (Sriram & Oster, 2012, p. 377). We are taught to do this in order to demonstrate value and relevance to the institutional mission, as well as impact on student development and learning. Using research in student affairs work has been continuously supported by researchers and practitioners (Sriram & Oster, 2012). The use of scholarship to inform practice has been critical in building frameworks in order to demonstrate contributions to educational mission and assist with assessing learning outcomes. Scholarship has also been used to build strong philosophical and educational foundations that have assisted in the identification of best practices and professional standards. The use of scholarship assists scholar-practitioners in building connections with faculty by addressing issues of teaching and learning through discussions of assessment, accountability, service learning, or the value of cocurricular education efforts on campus (Kidder, 2010). In this context, the Wabash National Study is an invaluable tool that can be used to support and identify the impact student affairs programs have on collegians.

As noted earlier, the idea of the scholar-practitioner is emphasized in many graduate programs and other professional contexts. Yet, the definition of scholar-practitioner has many dimensions and can be defined in several ways. The term "scholar-practitioner" has been used to describe a practice where the work of the professional student affairs practitioner and faculty member or researcher conducting scholarly research are integrated

NEW DIRECTIONS FOR STUDENT SERVICES • DOI: 10.1002/ss

into daily work (Jablonski, Mena, Manning, Carpenter, & Siko, 2006). Manning defined the scholar/practitioner as an individual whose "scholarship is a combination of original research but often includes reflective pieces about practice in the field" (Jablonski et al., 2006, p. 192). Manning continues the discussion about practitioner/scholars by stating, "Practitioner/scholars ... these folks are out in the field as administrators and educators. But they write and make contributions to the field in terms of reflection and research" (Jablonski et al., 2006, p. 192). These definitions are critical to understanding the complexities surrounding the conversations regarding scholar-practitioner. Regardless of whether one identifies as a scholar-practitioner or a practitioner-scholar, the foundational values of practice and scholarship are critical. Intentional integration of practice and scholarship (i.e., scholarship to inform practice and practice to inform scholarship) is an essential habit of mind. The scholar-practitioner is someone who values data and uses research findings to inform decision and policy making (Milem & Inkelas, 2009). It is a person who intentionally uses and engages in research within and for their practice. Scholar-practitioners understand the critical role research findings have in improving higher education as a whole. McClintock (2003) noted that scholarly practice is grounded in theory and research, included experimental knowledge, and was driven by personal values, commitment, and ethical conduct. Scholar-practitioners reflect on and assess the impact of their work. According to Bensimon, Polkinghorne, Bauman, and Vallejo (2004), the value of knowledge and taking action in the local context is a distinguishing state of mind. Benham (1996) added a problem-solving approach to scholarly practice and emphasized the role of scholar-practitioner as learning about or recognizing problems, examining them closely, and searching for productive solutions. These multiple understandings of scholar-practitioner enrich and complicate the meaning of this term.

As demonstrated earlier, notions regarding scholar-practitioner are complex and can take various meanings depending on context. Complicating these conversations are the ways in which there is concern about the possible divide between scholars and practitioners in the student affairs field (Blimling, 2001; Jablonski et al., 2006). The scholar-practitioner engages in research to improve effectiveness. A scholar-practitioner is described as an administrator who desires to engage in research within and for their practice. These administrators may be scholar-practitioners, practitioner-scholars, practitioners, or individuals who value research but struggle to engage in literature. The critical component is that these individuals value and engage with research in one way, shape, or form.

Working at the nexus of research and professional practice can be a struggle. Often at conflict is the need to focus on daily office management, supervision, and administrative work and using effective practices to improve services and programs. Balancing the administrative work and the work associated with staying up to date on, and using, current scholarship can be difficult (Bishop, 2010). This is the reality of the work of a scholar-practitioner. Understanding how to navigate this type of conflict is crucial to the success of a scholar-practitioner, as the conflict is both internal and external and can often feel difficult to control. Understanding ways in which one can be a scholar-practitioner includes both *habits of mind* and *habits of practice* that can be simultaneously demanding and fulfilling.

Intersections of Scholarship and Practice

As a practitioner, I am often asked by colleagues about the importance of putting theory into practice and using data to inform practice. At the core of the question is: "Why bother?" I am often reminded of the difficulty of putting theory into practice or using, even finding, relevant data to inform daily practice. Yet, research-driven practice is an essential component to being a productive and effective practitioner. It is important for student affairs professionals to demonstrate contributions to the advancement of the institutional mission, as well as the ways student affairs professionals contribute to conversations regarding assessment, accountability, service learning, and/or the value of cocurricular education efforts on campus.

Using Research to Demonstrate Impact.   To equip oneself with information is powerful. As more demands are placed on practitioners to demonstrate impact and contributions to the campus community, it is critical to understand how to engage with scholarship in a way that is both useful and powerful. The ability to explain how student affairs contributes to the academic mission of the institution is critical, particularly with demands for student affairs units to describe impact and contributions to student learning in a measureable way. The student affairs professional who has developed the skills of a scholar-practitioner has the ability to meet administrators and faculty on their own terms. Scholarship and evidence can be used in many different ways to legitimize student affairs work. It can be used to inform and guide practice such as development of mission, program development, policy, organizational structure, and so forth. It can also be used to justify initiatives, advocate for resources, and demonstrate overall impact on student learning and/or educational mission of the institution.

As budgets are increasingly scrutinized and demand to prove value of services and programs to a variety of stakeholders (including governing boards, administrators, faculty, and parents) increases, it is imperative to continue to engage the student affairs literature (Sriram & Oster, 2012) to demonstrate value and impact. As Bishop (2010) suggested, connections need to be made between what student affairs professionals do in their practice and the body of knowledge the profession is built upon. Current research suggests that there is a need for increased engagement in research among professionals (Sriram & Oster, 2012). Intentional steps need to be taken to help professionals (new and seasoned) understand the importance of reading current research for the sake of better practice.

Doing Research in a Local Context.   As noted by Bensimon et al. (2004) and Dean (2010), utilizing evidence to understand effectiveness in your local context can be a powerful way to hone your scholar-practitioner skills. Requests to demonstrate effectiveness and engage in assessment are increasing, and this is one way to bridge scholarship and practice (Dean, 2010; Mentkowski & Loacker, 2002). As Dean points out, one of the assets of scholar-practitioners is their knowledge of local contexts and cultures: student, staff, faculty, issues, structures, politics, and so forth. The practitioner understands the specific needs of one's own campus and the unique ways they conduct their professional work. Being immersed in our own institution's values and mission provides an opportunity for scholar-practitioners to focus on what matters. While not every practitioner may have developed skills in the area of assessment, they can partner with someone on campus who can assist with design, data collection, and analysis. The practitioner can contribute their wealth of knowledge about the student experience to the interpretation and use of evidence collected.

Using Scholarship to Inform Practice.   Does scholarship inform your practice? Does research inform daily practice? The foundation of these questions is intentionality. We can all find ways to engage scholarship in practice. In fact, we should do them as a matter of *good practice* (Dean, 2010). The "inner scholar" and "inner practitioner" can, and should, be in constant dialogue. Finding ways to integrate these two identities are critical to the success of the scholar-practitioner. Practicing and valuing evidence-based thinking and engaging others in process are critical skills that can be applied to the practice of educating students and improving institutions of higher education (Milem & Inkelas, 2009). As a profession, we can encourage the work of scholarly practice and evidence-based decision making. While scholars and practitioners may have different habits of mind (Kezar, 2000), scholar-practitioners integrate the best of both worlds. Such individuals have the ability to remove the dichotomy of practice and intellect. They are able to participate in the actions of both doing and knowing (Dean, 2010).

The difficulty is actually integrating scholarship with practice or "doing the work." One of the responsibilities we as practitioners have is interpreting the findings and suggestions and adapting them for our campus/local contexts. This work not only takes time and energy, more often than not it also takes resources, creativity, agency, and buy-in from key stakeholders. Having the ability to interpret data and develop and implement action plans places scholar-practitioners in a unique space. It is the space where research informs practice and can be used to justify, explain, and legitimize daily work.

NEW DIRECTIONS FOR STUDENT SERVICES • DOI: 10.1002/ss

Using the WNS in Practice. Results from the Wabash National Study can be valuable tools if used to create a foundation to inform daily practice. As a professional, I can use data associated with the WNS to demonstrate the ways in which programs and resources impact student learning. Data also provide a context for faculty and other administrators to understand how my work supports student learning and promotes diversity and the academic mission of the institution.

Questions around the value of relationship building and time spent with students can arise when relationship building is not seen as a value-added component of one's job. In Chapter 5 of this volume, Martin and McGee explained how the WNS data can be used to highlight the importance of student affairs professionals building intentional structured relationships. In my own work, this has led me to consider the ways I can create structured mentoring opportunities for students with professional staff members at my institution.

The WNS findings have been powerful tools when I have addressed multicultural issues on campus. As more institutions articulate the value of diversity and social justice in their missions and goals, it is important to understand the ways in which critical dialogues, educational programming, and relationships can be integrated and promote learning. As highlighted by Goodman and Bowman in Chapter 4 of this volume, diversity education needs to be framed as cognitive and psychosocial development opportunities. These opportunities should be promoted as opportunities to promote relationship building, critical thinking skills, and engagement with difference. In addition, findings from the WNS support the need for diverse interpersonal interaction and highlight that such experiences, in some cases, promote student learning and development. This argument, reframed for audience and campus context, can be powerful. As diversity education continues to be scrutinized, it is important to continue to explain and describe its impact on student learning. The use of data is an integral tool in this argument and can help bolster the arguments for why diversity matters and how diversity education positively impacts cognitive and psychosocial development.

A final way I have used findings from the WNS to reflect on my own practice is by considering the role of critical conversations in student affairs work. What is right? What is just? Conversations on these issues encourage moral and ethical development among students and can be difficult, uncomfortable, and, at times, dangerous. As Seifert noted in Chapter 2 of this volume, critical conversations are important interactions that assist in the development of moral reasoning. They are opportunities to engage with diverse perspectives and are essential in creating transformative learning environments. During a time of litigation and fear of retribution, there is a need to use research to ground arguments that support the need for critical conversations that may make individuals uncomfortable. This type of conversation encourages the exchange of ideas. It is during these conversations that understanding WNS findings can be powerful in supporting student-learning initiatives and in promoting ethical and moral development.

Using information found in the WNS can help frame conversations in the student affairs field that can redefine and/or clarify *how* work is done and create opportunities for further assessment of practices and work. It is critical for scholar-practitioners to understand how they can utilize the WNS data, and other data available to them, to build powerful arguments and support practices that promote student development and learning.

Critical Questions.   As greater demands are made for practitioners to adopt the scholar-practitioner model, it will be important for practitioners to continuously challenge themselves place research at the core of professional practice. One should explore questions such as:

- What should you be doing to stay on the cutting edge of your field?
- How is the role of scholar-practitioner important on your own campus? How is it important to you professionally?
- What resources do you have access to help you integrate scholarship into your practice?
- What are success strategies for scholar-practitioners?
- How do you incorporate scholarship/research/evidence into professional practice?

These questions broaden one's understanding of the role of the scholar-practitioner as well as help define professional goals and values.

In addition to the questions posed above, the question "What prevents practitioners from engaging in scholarly activities?" must be explored. This question is not meant to place blame, but rather to encourage one to explore barriers that might prevent practitioners from engaging in scholarly activity. Questions to ask to help identify challenges include:

- *Do you know how to engage in scholarly activity? If not, do you have access to resources to learn how to engage in these activities?* Not everyone knows how to engage in scholarly activity and how to integrate it into professional practice. What resources do you have available to you to help you develop these skills?
- *Do you have support to put resources toward scholarly activity and incorporate it in professional practice?* Resources, time, and support are critical to the success of scholar-practitioners: Support from supervisors, having time and resources to put toward scholarly activities, having administrative unit/institutional support, etc.
- *Is scholarly activity valued by your administrative unit?* If the administrative unit you work for does not support scholarly activity, it may be difficult to maintain the work of a scholar-practitioner. It is important to understand the values and goals of the unit. In addition, it will be vital

NEW DIRECTIONS FOR STUDENT SERVICES • DOI: 10.1002/ss

to understand how to gain buy-in and support if there is resistance to scholar-practitioner work.

- *Do barriers include lack of time or resources?* Barriers, including lack of time and other resources, can be difficult to overcome. Yet, with some creativity and support from peers and colleagues, they may be addressed in a manner that is relevant for both your administrative unit as well as your professional goals.
- *Is it difficult to find support from peers?* Do you find resistance from peers and colleagues when you talk about evidence-based practice? What does this mean for relationship building and collegial relationships? How does this impact the administrative unit culture and the work that you are trying to achieve?

These questions will help you understand what obstacles may prevent you and other practitioners from participating in scholarly activities.

Jablonski et al. (2006) discussed the challenges practitioners encounter trying to incorporate scholarship with practice:

> Most practitioners do not have time within their current positions to include research and writing. The 'tyranny of the immediate' impedes the ability of student affairs educators to engage in scholarship. What skills and knowledge do practitioners need to develop a scholarship agenda? What support, coaching, and job modifications create environments for practitioners to be successful? (Jablonski et al., 2006, p. 197)

The challenge of finding time, resources, and support is very real and can serve as barriers that prohibit practitioners from engaging in scholar-practitioner practices. However, it is important to identify these barriers and determine ways to overcome them rather than allow them to prevent you from participating in scholar-practitioner practices.

Final Thoughts

Scholarship and evidence-based practice are critical for effective student affairs practice. The scholar-practitioner exists in a space where research and practice inform each other and create a synergy: research informing practice, practice informing scholarship, and the many combinations. A scholar-practitioner understands the importance of practice and research informing each other and the need to ground work in theory and evidence and create measurements that demonstrate impact as well as explore phenomena.

The value of knowledge as a means to improve practice is essential. Understanding and centering research and scholarship in professional practice are important to the success of a scholar-practitioner. It is viewed as a way to legitimize, explain, and improve practice. The scholar-practitioner engages in research to improve practice or to develop best practices in administrative discipline. Scholar-practitioners utilize the research reports of others and use them to improve their own effectiveness and that of their staff or peers. The scholar-practitioner generates new knowledge not to convince a tenure committee that they have earned their place as a colleague but to continue to advance knowledge or practice in a field.

As discussed earlier, there are many ways in which a practitioner can integrate scholarly practice in daily work. One does not have to conduct original research to be considered a scholar-practitioner. The scholar-practitioner can find many relevant ways to engage in scholarly practice. These opportunities strengthen not only the "practitioner" skills but also sharpen and refine "scholarly" skills. These skills have the opportunity to interact and work in synergy. The scholar-practitioner has to learn how to hone these skills so they work together and create a framework that will allow for practice and intellect to converge and move toward creating informed practices, polices, decisions, and services that will improve higher education institutions.

For scholar-practitioners, multitasking has been a way of existence. It is a frame of mind. It includes navigating the realms of practitioner and scholar as well as having the ability to understand how to translate relevant research and data and incorporate it into daily practice. As I think about relevant skills, it takes the ability to understand how to integrate practice and scholarship and share the information in a meaningful way with key decision makers. This work takes mental agility as well dedication to both knowing and doing. The reality is that it is possible for a practitioner to be a scholar and a scholar to be a practitioner. It does not have to be a choice. It is a frame of mind and habit of practice that can help strengthen practice and broaden understanding of why we do the work we do and how we do it.

References

Benham, M. K. P. (1996). The practitioner-scholars' view of school changes: A case-based approach to teaching and learning. *Teaching and Teacher Education, 12*(2), 119–135.

Bensimon, E. M., Polkinghorne, D. E., Bauman, G. L., & Vallejo, E. (2004). Doing research that makes a difference. *Journal of Higher Education, 75*(1), 104–126.

Bishop, J. D. (2010). Becoming a scholar-practitioner: The road less traveled. *ACPA Developments, 8*(3). Retrieved from http://www.myacpa.org/article/becoming-scholar-practitioner-road-less-traveled

Blimling, G. S. (2001). Uniting scholarship and communities of practice in student affairs. *Journal of College Student Development, 42*(4), 381–396.

Dean, K. L. (2010). What defines a scholar practitioner? A way of thinking and doing. *ACPA Developments, 8*(2). Retrieved from http://www.myacpa.org/article/part-ii-scholar-practitioner-what-defines-scholar-practitioner-way-thinking-and-doing

Jablonski, M. A., Mena, S. B., Manning, K., Carpenter, S., & Siko, K. L. (2006). Scholarship in student affairs revisited: The summit on scholarship, March 2006. *NASPA Journal, 43*(4), 182–200.

Kezar, A. (2000). Higher education research at the millennium: Still trees without fruit? *Review of Higher Education, 23*(4), 443–468.

Kidder, R. (2010). Administrators engaging in the research process. *ACPA Developments*, *8*(1). Retrieved from http://www.myacpa.org/article/administrators-engaging-research-process

McClintock, C. (2003). Scholar practitioner model. *Encyclopedia of Distributed Learning.* Retrieved from http://knowledge.sagepub.com/view/distributedlearning/n134.xml

Mentkowski, M., & Loacker, G. (2002). Enacting a collaborative scholarship of assessment. In T. W. Banta & Associates (Eds.), *Building a scholarship of assessment*, 82–99. San Francisco, CA: Jossey-Bass.

Milem, J., & Inkelas, K. K. (2009, November). *Celebrating the mentor and mentee relationship.* Presidential panel session at the Association for the Study of Higher Education Conference, Vancouver, BC, Canada. Retrieved from http://www.ashe.ws/images/ASHE%20Prez%20Session%20mentor%20&%20mentee%20reflections.pdf

Sriram, R., & Oster, M. (2012). Reclaiming the "scholar" in scholar-practitioner. *Journal of Student Affairs Research and Practice*, *49*(4), 377–396.

V. LEILANI KUPO serves as the director of the Women's Resources and Research Center at University of California-Davis.

NEW DIRECTIONS FOR STUDENT SERVICES • DOI: 10.1002/ss

INDEX

AAC&U. *See* Association for American Colleges and Universities (AAC&U)

ACT. *See* American College Testing Program (ACT)

Adelman, C., 77

Ahren, C., 26–27

Ainsworth, S., 26

Allen, W. R., 37, 72

American Association for Higher Education, 50

American College Personnel Association (ACPA), 50

American College Testing Program (ACT), 7

American Council on Education (ACE), 49

Antonio, A., 26

Asel, A. M., 25–27, 83

Askew, J., 26

Assault on Diversity, The, 42

Association for American Colleges and Universities (AAC&U), 45

Association of Fraternity/Sorority Advisors (AFA) Executive Board, 23

Astin, A. W., 26–27, 38, 49, 51–52

Atlas, G., 27

At-risk students, WNS and, 77–85; academic experiences, 79–81; definition, 77; experiences with diversity for, 81–82; out-of-class experiences for, 82–83; overview, 77–78; student affairs practice, recommendations for, 83–85

Auvenshine, C. D., 25

Avalos, J., 51

Barber, J. P., 2, 3, 8–9, 11, 32, 42, 59–63, 75

Barnhardt, C., 14–15, 19

Bauman, G. L., 91, 93

Baxter Magolda, M. B., 8–9, 14–15, 19, 37, 39, 41–42, 60–64

Bebeau, M., 7, 13–14, 18

Benham, M. K. P., 91

Bensimon, E. M., 91, 93

Berrett, D., 10

Biddix, J. P., 27, 33

Birkenbolz, R. J., 27

Bishop, J. D., 92

Blaich, C. F., 9–10, 14, 16, 18–19, 21, 39–40, 79, 81–82

Blechschmidt, S., 26

Blimling, G. S., 50–51, 91

Bowman, N. A., 2, 15, 17, 37–41, 43–44, 48, 82, 94

Brand, J. A., 27

Braskamp, L. A., 72

Bray, G. B., 7

Bridges, B. K., 84

Buckley, J. A., 84

Bulger, S., 78

Bureau, D., 2, 23, 26–27, 32, 36

CAAP. *See* Collegiate Assessment of Academic Proficiency (CAAP)

Cacioppo, J., 7

Carini, R. M., 27

Carpenter, S., 4–5, 91, 96

Carroll, C. D., 77

Charmaz, K., 62

Chen, X., 77

Cho, E., 26

Choy, S. P., 77

Clayton-Pedersen, A. R., 37, 72

Cohen, E. R., 25

Cokorinos, L., 37, 42–43

Collegiate Assessment of Academic Proficiency (CAAP), 7, 25

Corbin, J., 62

Cultures and Traditions, 62, 64

Data-driven decision making: definition, 3–4 ; *vs.* research-driven practice, 4

Dean, K. L., 92–93

DeBard, R., 24

Defining Issues Test 2 (DIT2), 7, 13

DeGraw, J. E., 14–15, 19, 42

Developmentally effective experiences (DEEs), 9

Dey, E. L., 37

NEW DIRECTIONS FOR STUDENT SERVICES

ORDER FORM SUBSCRIPTION AND SINGLE ISSUES

DISCOUNTED BACK ISSUES:

Use this form to receive 20% off all back issues of *New Directions for Student Services*.
All single issues priced at **$23.20** (normally $29.00)

TITLE	ISSUE NO.	ISBN
_____	_____	_____
_____	_____	_____
_____	_____	_____

*Call 888-378-2537 or see mailing instructions below. When calling, mention the promotional code JBNND
to receive your discount. For a complete list of issues, please visit www.josseybass.com/go/ndss*

SUBSCRIPTIONS: (1 YEAR, 4 ISSUES)

☐ New Order   ☐ Renewal

U.S.	☐ Individual: $89	☐ Institutional: $311
CANADA/MEXICO	☐ Individual: $89	☐ Institutional: $351
ALL OTHERS	☐ Individual: $113	☐ Institutional: $385

*Call 888-378-2537 or see mailing and pricing instructions below.
Online subscriptions are available at www.onlinelibrary.wiley.com*

ORDER TOTALS:

Issue / Subscription Amount: $ _____

Shipping Amount: $ _____
(for single issues only – subscription prices include shipping)

Total Amount: $ _____

SHIPPING CHARGES:

First Item	$6.00
Each Add'l Item	$2.00

*(No sales tax for U.S. subscriptions. Canadian residents, add GST for subscription orders. Individual rate subscriptions must
be paid by personal check or credit card. Individual rate subscriptions may not be resold as library copies.)*

BILLING & SHIPPING INFORMATION:

☐ **PAYMENT ENCLOSED:** *(U.S. check or money order only. All payments must be in U.S. dollars.)*

☐ **CREDIT CARD:** ☐ VISA ☐ MC ☐ AMEX

Card number _____Exp. Date_____

Card Holder Name_____Card Issue # _____

Signature _____Day Phone_____

☐ **BILL ME:** *(U.S. institutional orders only. Purchase order required.)*

Purchase order # _____
Federal Tax ID 13559302 • GST 89102-8052

Name_____

Address_____

Phone_____ E-mail_____

Copy or detach page and send to: **John Wiley & Sons, One Montgomery Street, Suite 1200,
San Francisco, CA 94104-4594**

Order Form can also be faxed to: **888-481-2665**

PROMO JBNND

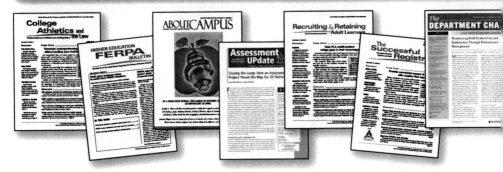